NEW
Grammar
Time
4

Teacher's Book

**Sandy Jervis, Maria Carling and
Gabrielle Pritchard**

PEARSON

Longman

Pearson Education Limited
Edinburgh Gate
Harlow
Essex CM20 2JE
England
and Associated Companies throughout the World.

www.longman.com

The right of Sandy Jervis, Maria Carling and Gabrielle Pritchard
to be identified as authors of this work has been asserted
by them in accordance with the Copyright, Designs and
Patents Act 1988.

First published 2001
This edition 2008

Teachers Book ISBN: 978-1-4058-5276-0

Printed in Malaysia, KHL (CTP)

Set in Ulissa 10pt

Cover by Mackerel Design.
Illustrations by Stephen May.
Designed and Project Managed by Starfish Design
Editorial and Project Management Ltd.

NEW Grammar Time 4

Teacher's Book

Contents

Introduction

Grammar Time is a series of grammar reference and practice books specifically designed for young learners from the age of eight upwards. **Grammar Time** can be used alongside any major coursebook. The aims and overall purpose of the series are:

- to present grammar in amusing, meaningful contexts, appropriate to the pupils' age and level.
- to help them understand new grammatical items by means of simple reference tables and explanations of key points.
- to help them assimilate the grammar by providing interesting, graded practice exercises.
- to provide opportunities to use the grammar communicatively in freer oral and/or written practice.

Grammar Time and the Common European Framework

The new editions of **Grammar Time** are closely correlated to the Common European Framework.

Grammar Time	Language level	Common European Framework	Cambridge ESOL
1	Beginners		Starters
2	False beginners	A1	Movers
3	Elementary	A2	Flyers, KET
4	Pre-Intermediate	B1	PET
5	Intermediate	B1+ (towards B2)	

Grammar Time components

The components of the course are:
- a Pupils' Book
- a Teacher's Resource Book with answer keys and additional photocopiable activities
- a Multi-ROM containing recorded material from the Pupils' Book that can be played on a CD player for use in the classroom; and extra practice exercises for the learners to do at home on their computers.

Grammar Time syllabus progression

The order in which grammatical items are introduced in **Grammar Time** follows the typical progression of most coursebooks. However, it is possible to select units in any order which is relevant and appropriate to the particular needs of your language classroom.

Organisation of Grammar Time 4 Pupils' Book

The main part of the book consists of:
- twenty-five core units
- five revision units called 'Use your English'

Additional reference material at the end of the book consists of:
- spelling rules
- unit by unit wordlist

Grammar Time Characters

There are recurring characters in *Grammar Time 3-5:* **Harry Banks, Beth MacKenzie, Peter** and **Lucy Hardy**. They all go to the same school – Peter and Harry are in the same class, Beth and Lucy are in the class below them.

- Harry is 12 years old. He is the editor of *'TeenLink'*, the school magazine. He loves basketball and watching DVDs with his friends.
- Beth is 11 years old. She's an assistant editor on *'TeenLink'* and is a keen reporter. She's very intelligent and has lots of good ideas for the magazine.
- Peter is Harry's best friend. He's 12 years old. He loves sport and enjoys teasing his little sister, Lucy.
- Lucy is 11 years old. She's artistic and very strong-minded.
- Cosmo and Bella are Harry's cats, although they spend a lot of time at Peter and Lucy's house.

Core units

Each core unit is organised in the following way.

Presentation

Motivating and memorable content facilitates the acquisition of language. In **Grammar Time 4**, grammar is presented in context through cartoons featuring the four main characters, the two cats and their friends. Pupils can easily identify with the varied and amusing situations the characters find themselves in.

Care has been taken so that larger "chunks" of grammar are broken down to make them more manageable for young learners. In **Grammar Time 4**, units vary in length according to the language item introduced. In Unit 4, for instance, which deals with the present perfect, the first three pages present and practise the positive, negative and question forms of the present perfect only. Exercises 7 and 8 highlight and practise the difference between *have/has been* and *have/has gone*. Exercises 9 and 10 focus on freer practice of the present perfect for talking about experiences ,and exercises 11 and 12 focus on the difference between the past simple and the present perfect, bringing both forms together and reinforcing the work done in Unit 2. The final exercise in Unit 4 provides personalised practice. This gives you some freedom to adapt the pace according to the needs of each individual class, choosing either to break down the unit into two or even three different lessons, or to deal with the whole unit at one go.

Grammar reference tables and explanations

The grammar reference tables help focus the learners' attention on the new grammatical items in a visually memorable way. Students are often asked to complete the tables themselves, using language extracted from the presentation cartoons.

Following the tables, is a Grammar Box, with explanations of form and use, which provides further clear examples of the grammar in context.

The tables and explanations appear together before the practice section. This makes it easy for pupils to refer to them while working through the exercises.

Exercises

The controlled practice exercises that follow each presentation are carefully graded to ensure that new language can be easily consolidated. They aim to recycle known vocabulary rather than introduce a large number of new lexical items, which would only serve to confuse and distract the pupils. The cartoon characters often appear in the exercises to provide realistic contexts for the grammatical items.

Each unit ends with a writing exercise, so that learners can put the new language they have learnt into use. Learners are given a clear model to follow and are then guided through the process of producing their own written work.

'Use your English' revision units

There are five revision units in the book. They allow for regular consolidation of the language presented and practised so far. The tasks aim to provide realistic and communicative contexts for the language to make it more memorable. Again, the lexis used is familiar to the learner.

Reference material

At the end of book, there are spelling rules for plural nouns, the third person singular (he, she, it) and verbs + -ing.

These provide a fast and simple way to review or revise these grammar areas.

Wordlist

This contains key lexical items from each unit. Your pupils may want to write in a translation of each word in their own language. They can use this for reference at home and for revision purposes.

For you, this list proves a preview of which words your pupils will need to know to be able to work alone on a unit. It can help you decide what key vocabulary to pre-teach before the Presentation.

Useful tips

Presentation

One of the main advantages of this series is its use of recurring cartoon characters which present grammar through amusing stories.

You can start off by asking pupils to look at the pictures and say what they think is happening. Depending on the linguistic level and perception of their class, you might find it useful to pre-teach key lexical items that appear in the presentation (using the wordlist if necessary).

You can ask pupils to repeat parts of the dialogue, and allow pupils to comment on the stories and give their opinions.

Follow-up ideas

- Pupils can act out the dialogues in class immediately.
- Pupils can be assigned to learn the lines of one of the characters for homework and act out the dialogues in the next lesson without books.
- You could write the dialogue on the board, leaving out key grammatical items, then ask pupils to fill them in.
- Pupils may be encouraged to write their own version of the story making any desirable changes (this can be done in class with the teacher as a resource; pupils then vote for the best version).

Grammar reference tables and explanations

It is advisable for you to go through these in class, before pupils work on the exercises. Pupils can be asked to read the items in the tables aloud (in chorus and individually) to familiarise themselves with pronunciation and stress. You can ask them to supply further examples based on the tables.

Draw your pupils' attention to any additional explanations, and make certain that they understand, adding extra examples on the board if you wish.

When this is done, pupils could be asked to go back to the presentation and circle, underline or highlight all grammatical items in focus.

Controlled practice exercises

The simple instructions and examples provided make all exercises suitable for homework. However, it is always advisable to do a sufficient number of them in class, where you can prompt, help and advise. If necessary, do more than one item as an example and ask pupils to work through the rest of the activity individually or, preferably, in pairs.

Pupils should be encouraged to ask questions if they are in difficulty. You can usually guide them towards finding the answer on their own by looking back at the presentation and tables.

When it is time for checking, it is a good idea to encourage the rest of the class to say whether a particular answer given is acceptable or not, rather than accepting or correcting immediately. Multiple choice exercises or those which require a choice between two words (e.g. *was* or *were*), make them suitable for "voting" – that is, pupils are asked to put their hands up to choose one of the answers (the majority is usually right).

'Use your English' revision units

The 'Use your English' revision units are best done in class, as they contain speaking exercises as well as written exercises.

Teacher's Resource Book

This Teacher's Resource Book contains answer keys to all the exercises in the Pupils' Book, as well as additional photocopiable activities with teaching notes and answer keys where applicable.

Photocopiable activities

There is one photocopiable activity sheet for each unit in the Pupils' Book. The activities consist of games, and pair or groupwork activities to activate the language practised in the unit in a lively and interesting way. This provides another opportunity to recycle the grammar and build your pupils' confidence in using the language.

The teaching notes explain how to use each activity and answers are provided where necessary.

Multi-ROM / CD-ROM

The Multi-ROM / CD-ROM packaged with each Pupils' Book contains extra practice exercises and games which can be done on a home computer. For each unit, there are up to five extra exercises as well as a final game to make learning fun. There are also five revision units for further consolidation. Only vocabulary that has been seen in the Pupils' Book is used, to facilitate pupils' understanding and allow them to focus on the grammar.

Key to the Pupils' Book

Unit 1

1

You / We / They   do
He / She / It   do

I   am
He / She / It   's
You / We / They   are
I   'm not
He / She / It   is not
We / You / They   are not

Is he / she / it   going?

3
1. goes
2. doesn't eat
3. do your cousins live
4. writes
5. Do your parents work
6. do you get up
7. don't go

4
1. 'm trying
2. aren't having
3. are you laughing
4. Is that girl talking
5. isn't studying
6. is writing

5
1. at the moment
2. every day
3. at the moment
4. every day
5. every day
6. at the moment

6
1. usually edits *Teenlink*; he is listening to his new CD.
2. usually does homework; she is watching a film on TV.
3. usually plays football; he is reading a book.
4. usually goes to the gym; she is visiting a friend.
5. usually studies Spanish; she is writing a story.
6. usually runs in the park; he is cooking dinner.

8
1. loves
2. are you looking
3. Do you remember
4. I'm watching
5. hates

6. I'm talking
7. are you doing
8. I don't understand

9
1. are you doing
2. I'm making
3. I'm going
4. Do you need
5. doesn't like
6. don't understand
7. 's waiting
8. 's reading
9. doesn't know

10
1. is staying
2. am not working
3. am just enjoying
4. has
5. usually gets up
6. runs
7. spends
8. don't usually have
9. am taking
10. is teaching
11. love

Unit 2

1
called
did not
No, I / you / he / she / it / we / they did not.

3

dropped	came
liked	forgot
stayed	kept
studied	knew
tidied	swam
travelled	took
tried	understood
	wrote

4
1. taught
2. gave
3. phoned
4. came
5. were
6. started
7. left
8. moved

5

1 They didn't go to a restaurant. They went to an internet café.
2 She didn't send him a letter. She sent him an e-mail.
3 He didn't buy a new computer last month. He bought a printer.
4 We didn't give him a book for his birthday. We gave him a CD-ROM.
5 Maria didn't download a game from their website. She downloaded some photographs.
6 He didn't give us his phone number. He gave us his e-mail address.

6

1 was
2 was
3 watched
4 went
5 had
6 visited
7 bought
8 ate
9 took
10 interviewed
11 didn't go
12 stayed
13 didn't come out
14 stopped

7

1 Did / stay   No, she didn't. She went to the park.
2 Did / like   Yes, she did.
3 Did / buy   Yes, he did.
4 Did / eat   No, he didn't. Peter ate six toffee apples.
5 Did / talk   Yes, she did.
6 Did / go   No, they didn't.

8

1 Where did they go?
2 What time did you get up on Sunday?
3 Why did he leave?
4 When did she call you?
5 Where were you at 8 o'clock?
6 How many tickets did you get?
7 What did Tom say?

9 I / You / He / She / It / We / They didn't use to play tennis.
No, I / You / He / She / It / We / They   didn't.

11

1 used to be
2 used to work
3 didn't use to drink

4 Did Tommy use to cry
5 used to travel
6 did you use to do
7 used to go
8 didn't use to like

12

1 She didn't use to have long hair twenty years ago, but she has long hair now.
2 She used to listen to rock music twenty years ago, but she doesn't now.
3 She didn't use to play chess twenty years ago, but she does now.
4 She used to go to parties twenty years ago, but she doesn't now.
5 She didn't use to drive a car twenty years ago, but she does now.
6 She didn't use to get up early twenty years ago, but she does now.

13

1 used to live
2 used to hunt
3 used to live
4 used to travel
5 used to make
6 used to fight
7 used to move
8 used to eat

14

1 talked
2 didn't have
3 had
4 carried
5 wanted
6 scratched
7 sent
8 had wrote
9 arrived
10 sat
11 watched

15

1 Walt Disney was an extraordinary man.
2 He had a great talent...
3 He studied drawing and photography...
4 Walt went to Hollywood and soon he became successful.
5 Roy Disney, Walt's brother, was his business manager.
6 Walt made the first cartoon film...
7 He produced Pinocchio...
8 Walt built...
9 Disneyland opened in 1955.
10 Walt Disney died in Los Angeles in 1966.

Unit 3

1 I / He / She / It was not (wasn't) walking.
We / You / They weren't walking.

Was I / he / she / it playing?
No, I / he / she / it wasn't.
Yes, you / we / they were.

3
1 Tanya wasn't listening to music.
2 Bill was doing his homework.
3 Ray and Bob weren't watching TV.
4 Tanya was having dinner.
5 Ray and Bob were listening to music.
6 Bill wasn't sleeping.
7&8 Students' own answers.

4
1 Lucy was reading a book.
2 Mrs Hardy was talking on the phone.
3 Peter and Harry were watching TV.
4 Mr Hardy was washing the car.
5 Beth and Bella were playing.
6 Cosmo was eating his dinner.

5
1 Was Cosmo playing with a toy mouse?
No, he wasn't. He was eating his dinner.
2 Was Lucy watching TV?
No, she wasn't. She was reading a book.
3 Was Mrs Hardy washing the car?
No, she wasn't. She was talking on the phone.
4 Were Peter and Harry doing their homework?
No, they weren't. They were watching TV.
5 Was Mr Hardy drinking tea?
No, he wasn't. He was washing the car.
6 Was Beth listening to music?
No, she wasn't. She was playing with Bella.

6
1 Were you working
2 wasn't
3 was watching
4 were studying
5 were getting
6 Was Suzie talking
7 wasn't talking to me
8 was singing
9 are the boys going
10 was tidying

7 He was watching TV
They were talking

While I was having breakfast
While we were waiting for the bus

9
1 was getting
2 went
3 Was it raining
4 came
5 fell
6 phoned

10
1 were waiting; got
2 was getting; heard
3 was living; met
4 were you doing; rang
5 saw; were going
6 was making; cut

11
1 when
2 While
3 when
4 while
5 while
6 when
7 while
8 When

12
1 Started; finished
2 Were you studying; called
3 were walking; saw
4 got up; had; went
5 was having; was writing
6 closed; took off; sat down
7 lost; was swimming
8 was doing; was having

13
1 was walking
2 thought
3 was standing
4 saw
5 were carrying
6 held
7 thanked
8 carried
9 went
10 was looking
11 remembered
12 fainted
13 were carrying

14
1 were
2 Did
3 was
4 Were
5 When
6 Did

15

1 drove
2 parked
3 walked
4 told
5 was driving
6 shouted
7 stopped
8 got
9 saw
10 was running
11 arrested
12 was paying
13 got into
14 drove
15 saw
16 ran
17 remembered
18 decided
19 was paying
20 saw

Use Your English 1

1

1 doesn't want
2 is Betty crying?
3 Do you lik
4 Am not having
5 Don't need
6 Are staying
7 Does your mum usually finish

2

1 She bought a birthday present for Peter.
2 She didn't call Harry.
3 She wrote an article for Teenlink.
4 She didn't go to the supermarket.
5 She downloaded Harry Walter's new song.
6 She didn't tidy her room.
7 She didn't wash her new jeans.
8 She met Peter at the station at six o'clock.

3

1 used to live
2 used to listen
3 didn't use to have
4 didn't use to go out
5 used to play
6 did you use to do

4

1 were you doing; phoned; was getting
2 Were Pete and Emma waiting; got; were; was
3 broke; was palying; told
4 Was Carl going; saw; wasn't; was talking
5 walked; were reading; did Mrs Cooper say
6 rang; was having; picked up

5

1 'm
2 did
3 was
4 are
5 ago
6 is
7 do

Unit 4

1

I / You / We / They ('ve)
He / She / It has ('s)
I / You / We / They (haven't)
He / She / It has not

Have I /we / you / they climbed / driven?
Yes, I / you / we / they have. / No, I / you / we / they haven't.
Has he / she / it climbed / driven?
Yes, he / she / it has. / No, he / she / it hasn't.

3

1 driven
2 sent
3 got
4 caught
5 let
6 been
7 met
8 eaten
9 fallen
10 swum
11 taught
12 found
13 written
14 known
15 cost

4

1 's bought
2 's sent
3 has brought
4 hasn't checked
5 haven't decorated
6 haven't blown
7 has made
8 has borrowed

5

1 Has Beth broken her sunglasses?   Yes, she has.
2 Has she bought a new CD?   Yes, she has.
3 Has she drunk her lemonade?   Yes, she has.
4 Has she eaten her sandwich?   Yes, she has.
5 Has she written a letter?   Yes, she has.
6 Has she posted the letter?   No, she hasn't.
7 Has she done well in her Maths test?   Yes, she has.
8 Has she finished her homework?   No, she hasn't.

6

1	Where have you put my car keys?	c
2	What has Mum cooked for dinner?	e
3	How much orange juice have you drunk?	a
4	Where has he parked the car?	b
5	What have you bought for Lee's birthday?	f
6	How many photos have you downloaded?	d

8

1 been
2 gone
3 gone
4 gone
5 been
6 gone
7 been
8 gone

9

1 have done
2 I haven't done
3 Haven't finished
4 Have you ever seen
5 Have seen
6 Have never been
7 Have you ever flown
8 Haven't
9 Have you ever seen
10 Haven't

10

1 the longest e-mail I've ever written
2 the best book I've ever written
3 the most boring story I've ever heard
4 the funniest person I've ever met
5 the most beautiful country we've ever visited
6 the best meal I've ever had
7 the worst photo I've ever seen
8 the fastest car he's ever driven

12

1 Have you met
2 I met
3 have never tried
4 took
5 Have you ever been
6 haven't
7 went
8 saw
9 have never seen
10 saw

13

1 have ever met
2 has done
3 has travelled
4 has visited

5 has been
6 has promised
7 has gone

14

Students' own answers.

Unit 5

1

1 He has just phoned.
2 We've already done our homework.
3 The football match hasn't started yet.
4 They haven't left yet.
5 Has she come back yet?
6 Have they gone home yet?
7 How long has he been in his room?
8 How long have they lived here?
9 They haven't called for days.
10 We haven't seen them since Monday.

3

1 already
2 yet
3 just
4 yet
5 already
6 just
7 yet
8 already

4

1 She's just left.
2 I've just bought a new computer.
3 Dave and Becky have just moved to Brighton.
4 I have just told Kim about the picnic.
5 I've just had one.
6 We've just come back from our holiday.

5

1 He's already tidied his room.
2 He hasn't bought a present for his Mum yet.
3 He's already cleaned the garage.
4 He's already watered the plants.
5 He hasn't phoned Peter yet.
6 He's already done the shopping.
7 He hasn't written the report for *Teenlink* yet.
8 He hasn't washed Dad's car yet.

6

1 since
2 for
3 for
4 since
5 for
6 since
7 since
8 for

7
1 already
2 How long
3 for
4 yet
5 since
6 just
7 already
8 How long

8
1 Their train hasn't arrived yet.
2 Sam hasn't phoned since Monday.
3 Trevor has already gone home.
4 It hasn't rained for months.
5 How long has Kathy been asleep?
6 Have you been to the shops yet?
7 Mark has just come back from France.
8 We haven't had breakfast yet.

10
1 two weeks ago
2 for a week
3 two weeks ago
4 for a week
5 for a week
6 two weeks ago

11
1 has broken; broke
2 have lost; lost
3 have sold; sold
4 have gone; went
5 have done; did
6 have bought; bought

12
1 has appeared
2 acted
3 was
4 appeared
5 didn't speak
6 has travelled
7 has never flown
8 has been
9 lost
10 went
11 found
12 went
13 painted
14 was
15 has painted

13
1 have
2 already
3 yet

4 done
5 just
6 did
7 have
8 since
9 went
10 for

14
1 Keira played her first role on TV when she was seven years old.
2 In 2001 she learnt how to...
3 She played football...
4 She became world famous...
5 She has taken part in...
6 She has already appeared...
7 She has not moved to ...
8 She has just finished filming...

Unit 6

I / You / He / She / It / We / They had gone / finished / called.
I / You / He / She / It / We / They had not gone / finished / called.
Had I / you / he / she / it / we / they gone/ finished / called?
Yes, I / you / he / she / it / we / they had.
No, I / you / he / she / it / we / they hadn't.

3
1 had left
2 hadn't stopped
3 had gone
4 hadn't met
5 hadn't brought
6 had / n't finished
7 hadn't slept
8 had taken

4
1 He had picked up Rocco's suit from the cleaner's.
2 He hadn't bought any flowers.
3 He had cleaned Rocco's shoes.
4 He hadn't washed the car.
5 He hadn't ironed Rocco's shirt.
6 He had been to the supermarket.

5
1 Their train left.
2 I went to bed.
3 We cleaned the house.
4 Ken had breakfast.
5 I met Kate's brother.
6 The guests left.

6
1 went; had spent
2 had just moved; met
3 had just finished; rang
4 had; washed
5 found; had bought
6 got; had already started
7 had already had; arrived
8 locked; left

7
Students' own answers.

8
1 she got up late because she'd forgotten to set the alarm clock the night before.
2 She didn't have a clean T-shirt to wear because her Mum had put all her T-shirts in the wash.
3 When she arrived at the bus stop, the school bus had left.
4 She didn't do well because she hadn't studied for it.
5 By the time Lucy put the phone down, the soap opera had finished.
6 When she woke up, the kitchen had filled with smoke.
7 She had called the fire brigade when she remembered the toast.

Use Your English 2

1
1 Have you ever been; have been
2 has Mum put
3 have cleaned; haven't finished
4 has Tom Brown written; have ever read
5 has never tried; Has he ever eaten
6 have made; Have you bought

2
1 Peter's just done his homework.
2 Harry's already checked his e-mails.
3 Beth hasn't done her homework yet.
4 Lucy and Sophie have already had lunch.
5 Peter hasn't tidied his room yet.
6 Beth has just finished her school project.
7 Lucy and Sophie haven't checked their e-mails yet.

3
1 since
2 for
3 since
4 for
5 since
6 for
7 since
8 for

4
1 B
2 A
3 C
4 A
5 B
6 A
7 C

5
1 had already gone; phoned
2 went; had done
3 got; had left
4 had just finished; rang
5 had already had; got up
6 had learnt; was
7 had just come; met
8 arrived; had escaped

Unit 7

1
I am / 'm going to watch a DVD.
We / You / They are going to watch a DVD.
He / She / It is not / isn't going to watch a DVD.

Am I going to watch a DVD?
Yes, I am. / No, I'm not.
Are we / you / they going to watch a DVD?
Yes, we / you / they are. / No, we / you / they aren't.
Is he / she / it going to watch a DVD?
Yes, he / she / it is. / No, he / she / it isn't.

3
1 You'll feel
2 I won't know
3 Will Amy like
4 you'll have
5 Harry won't let
6 our team will win

4
1 I'll get
2 I'll phone
3 I'll be
4 I'll ask
5 I'll open
6 I won't tell

5
1 It's going to be
2 's going to knock
3 's going to turn
4 's going to have
5 's going to land
6 's going to take

6
1 is going to have
2 aren't going to come
3 are you going to tidy
4 are going to move
5 Is your brother going to sell
6 I'm not going to lend
7 are going to stay
8 'm not going to tell

7
1 I'll get
2 I'm going to buy
3 'll help
4 are going to visit
5 'll look
6 Are you going to watch

8
1 are you doing
2 are going
3 am meeting
4 I'm helping
5 is coming
6 isn't coming
7 are going

9
1 is coming
2 is helping
3 are taking
4 are going
5 'll do
6 'll be
7 'll call

10

1	Are	6	will
2	not	7	will
3	am	8	I
4	is	9	are
5	are	10	will

11

1	b	5	c
2	c	6	b
3	a	7	c
4	a	8	a

12
1 we're going to see
2 'm going to train
3 'll do
4 Are you going to continue
5 'm going to study
6 'm going to open
7 'll give
8 'm spending

13
Students' own answers.

Unit 8

1
He can't play the violin.
She couldn't speak French when she was five.
She won't be able to join us tomorrow.

Can you play the violin?
Could he speak French when he was five?
Will they be able to join us tomorrow?

You can't use my computer.
Could you open the door?

3
1 can't
2 Could
3 Couldn't
4 Can
5 Can't
6 could

4
1 will be able to answer
2 won't be able
3 will be able to lend
4 Will you be able to finish
5 will be able to drive
6 won't be able to join

5
1 Ian couldn't draw two years ago. He can't draw now. He will be able to draw when he is five.
2 Ian couldn't ride a bike two years ago. He can't ride a bike now. He will be able to ride a bike when he is five.
3 Ian couldn't read two years ago. He can't read now. He won't be able to read when he is five.
4 Ian couldn't write two years ago. He can't write now. He will be able to write when he is five.
5 Ian couldn't swim two years ago. He can't swim now. He will be able to swim when he is five.

7
1 Can
2 could; can
3 Could
4 could; can't
5 Can
6 Could
7 Can; can't
8 Can

8
1 Could you open the door for me, please?
2 Can you help me with my homework, please?
3 Could I use the phone, please?

4 Can you be quiet, please?
5 Could you speak more slowly, please?
6 Can I borrow an umbrella, please?

10
1 has to get up
2 have to go
3 had to take
4 have to buy
5 has to wear
6 will have to ask

11
1 must
2 had to
3 must
4 must
5 had to
6 must
7 had to
8 had to

12
1 don't have to
2 don't have to
3 mustn't
4 doesn't have to
5 mustn't
6 don't have to
7 mustn't
8 mustn't

13
1 must   6 must
2 can   7 can
3 can't   8 must
4 mustn't   9 can
5 can

14
1 c   5 c
2 c   6 b
3 b   7 a
4 a   8 b

15
Students' own answers.

Unit 9

1 We may go to the party.
He might not like the painting.
You could meet us there.
He must be in the modern art room.
He can't be there.
You shouldn't worry so much.
Should I phone him?

3
1 may not
2 could
3 may not
4 may not
5 could
6 may not
7 could
8 could

4
1 might not go
2 might need
3 might be
4 might not buy
5 might not pass
6 might know
7 might not wear
8 might rain

5
1 must
2 can't
3 must
4 must
5 must
6 can't
7 can't
8 must

6
1 must
2 may
3 may
4 might
5 must
6 can't
7 must
8 might

7
1 should
2 should
3 should
4 should
5 shouldn't
6 should
7 shouldn't
8 should

8
1 must
2 can't
3 can't
4 mustn't
5 could

6 can't
7 can't
8 might

9
Students' own answers.

Unit 10

3
1 I'll
2 Shall I
3 Shall I
4 I'll
5 Shall I
6 I'll
7 I'll
8 Shall I

4
1 Shall I
2 Would you like
3 Shall I
4 Would you like
5 Shall I
6 I'll
7 shall I
8 Would you like

5
1 Would you like
2 Let's
3 Shall we
4 Would you like
5 Shall we
6 Let's
7 Shall we
8 Would you like

6
1 Why don't we stay / How about staying at home tonight?
2 Why don't we make / How about making some sandwiches?
3 Why don't we watch / How about watching a DVD?
4 Why don't we go / How about going to the beach?
5 Why don't we have / How about having a party?
6 Why don't we download / How about downloading the photos from the Internet?
7 Why don't we play / How about playing *Monopoly*?
8 Why don't we eat / How about eating out tonight?

7
1 How about
2 invite
3 shall

4 go
5 could
6 What about
7 Shall we
8 could

8
1 Can
2 Why
3 could
4 How
5 Would
6 I'll

9
1 Let's go for a walk.
  Why don't we visit a friend?
  Shall we play football in the park?
  How about catching the bus into town?
2 Can I do something for you?
  Shall I take you home?
  Would you like a glass of water?

10
Suggested answers:
  Would you like a drink?
  Why don't we go out and make a snowman?
  Let's go out and make a snowman.
  Shall I open it for you?
  Shall we / Why don't we go to the beach?
  Let's go to the beach!

Unit 11

1 When I get a new CD, we always listen to it together.
  If you pull out that plug, you will cut off the electricity.
  If he doesn't invite me to the party, I won't go.

  If I were you, I wouldn't work so hard.

3
1 hide
2 don't get up
3 phones
4 don't tidy
5 isn't
6 feel
7 Does Mrs Richards look after
8 gets

5
1 passes
2 'll talk
3 don't finish
4 will be

5 don't hurry
6 will send
7 doesn't come
8 don't leave
9 won't go
10 will phone

6
1 leave; might get
2 will stay; doesn't feel
3 ask; will help
4 see; don't tell
5 Will your dad be; finds out
6 may miss; don't hurry
7 finish; can meet
8 are; won't go
9 don't make; will get
10 Call ; need

7
1 will be
2 forgets
3 am not
4 save
5 finish
6 stay up
7 will be
8 have
Students complete the sentences with their own answers.

9
1 didn't live
2 didn't need
3 would get
4 were
5 had
6 happened
7 would visit
8 wouldn't help

10
1 had; 'd phone
2 wouldn't lie
3 didn't have; would stay
4 would get; had
5 wasn't / weren't; would buy
6 didn't like; wouldn't call
7 would you say; asked
8 was / were; wouldn't spend

11
1 'd take
2 'd take
3 caught
4 'd light
5 was / were

6 'd keep
7 'd have
8 could take
9 'd choose
10 'd carry

12 I wish I was / were famous.
I wish + was / were Unit 11

13
1 I wish I didn't have a headache.
2 I wish I wasn't ill.
3 I wish Mum was here.
4 I wish I didn't have to stay in bed.
5 I wish I could go to the park.
6 I wish I could eat some ice cream.

14
1 didn't have
2 could go
3 could come
4 would have
5 would be
6 could do
7 had
8 wasn't

15
Students' own answers.

Use Your English 3

1
1 c
2 b
3 a
4 a

2
1 is
2 to
3 will
4 are
5 'm
6 going
7 'll

3
1 Can
2 won't
3 Shall
4 don't have to
5 could
6 can't

4
1 had
2 hadn't lied
3 we watch
4 don't leave
5 I'd
6 like
7 could help
8 going

5
Students' own answers.

Unit 12

1

Regular plurals	Irregular plurals
books	women
dresses	feet
countries	fish
wolves	

There are two sandwiches in the fridge.
Your hair is longer than mine.

Where are my sunglasses?
I bought two pairs of jeans.

3
1 students; boys; girls.
2 loaves; tomatoes
3 glasses; plates
4 feet; minutes
5 strawberries; cherries; hours
6 people; cousins
7 knives; forks
8 Deer; forests

4

-s	-es	-ies	-ves	Irregular
answers	beaches	babies	knives	children
monkeys	classes	dictionaries	leaves	fish
places	foxes	ladies	loaves	people
radios	tomatoes	libraries	shelves	teeth
restaurants	wishes	parties	wives	women

5

month	C	oil	U	magazine	C
air	U	skirt	C	money	U
friend	C	milk	U	family	C
photo	C	help	U	rice	U
love	U	leaf	C	cotton T-shirt	C
meat	U	bread	U		

6
1 are
2 there's
3 pyjamas

4 those
5 glasses
6 piece

8
1 the
2 an; a; The; the
3 a
4 the
5 an
6 The
7 a
8 An; a; a

9
1 The
2 (–); (–)
3 (–); the
4 The; (–)
5 (–); the
6 (–); (–)
7 (–); the
8 (–); (–)
9 (–)
10 The; (–)

10
1 (–)
2 (–)
3 an
4 An
5 (–)
6 (–)
7 The
8 the
9 (–)

11
a
2 (–)
3 the
4 the
5 an
6 (–)
7 the
8 the
9 (–)
10 the
11 (–)
12 (–)

12
1 a
2 birthday
3 home
4 Biology
5 the station
6 South Street

13
1 the
2 the
3 the
4 the
5 (–)
6 the
7 a
8 a
9 an
10 (–)
11 the
12 the
13 the

14
1 a
2 men
3 glasses

4   faces
5   mice
6   the
7   An
8   the
9   Thieves
10   money
11   an
12   a
2   men
3   glasses
13   a
5   mice
14   the
3   men

15
Students' own answers.

Unit 13

1   We've got no biscuits.
We haven't got any cake.
Have we got any cake?

How many presents did Peter get?
Peter got a lot of / lots of presents.

How much money has Lucy got?
Lucy's got a lot of / lots of money.

3
1	any	5	some
2	some	6	no
3	no	7	any
4	any	8	some

4
1   somebody
2   anything
3   anybody
4   somewhere
5   nobody
6   anywhere
7   something
8   nothing

6
1   How much; A lot!
2   How many; A lot!
3   How much; Not much.
4   How much; A lot!
5   How many; One.
6   How much; Not much.
7   How many; Not many.
8   How many; Fifteen.

7
1   a few
2   a few
3   a little
4   a few
5   a little
6   a little
7   a little
8   a little

8
1   How much
2   a lot of / lots of
3   much
4   How many
5   many
6   a lot of / lots of
7   How many
8   a lot of / lots of
9   How much
10   How many
11   much
12   a few

9
Suggested answer:

Dear Diary

I had a [1] horrible day today First, I went to the park with my friends.

There [2] weren't many people there because the weather was [3] terrible. There [4] were a lot of dark clouds and it was really [5] cold. We [6] didn't have any ice cream, we played [7] a few games and then we decided to go to the cinema.

There were [8] a lot of people so we [9] spent [10] a lot of time in the queue. It was a science fiction film, but it [11] didn't have many special effects. It was really [12] terrible!

Unit 14

1   Both of them are pretty.

All of them show brothers and sisters.
Neither of them was interesting.

3
1   Neither
2   Both
3   Both
4   neither
5   Both
6   Neither
7   Neither
8   both

4
1 Neither of them...
2 Both of them...
3 Both of them...
4 Neither of them...
5 Neither of them...
6 Both of them...
7 Neither of them...

5
1 all
2 None
3 None
4 All
5 None
6 All
7 All
8 None

6
1 All
2 all
3 none
4 all
5 none
6 All

8
1 ones
2 one
3 ones
4 one; one
5 one
6 ones
7 ones
8 one

9
1 all
2 one
3 Both
4 Neither
5 Which
6 one
7 one
8 ones

10
Suggested answer:

I've got two good friends, Sophie and Beth. ¹ Both of them are very pretty, as you can see in the photo. ² Beth is the girl with the brown hair and Sophie is the blonde one. ³ We all go to the same school but we aren't in the same class. Beth is in my brother's class.

⁴ We all love music and listen to CDs together all the time. We often say that we should start our own pop group:

⁵ both of the girls have got very good singing voices and Sophie can play the piano. I can't sing but I can play the violin. Unfortunately, ⁶ neither of them thinks I'm good so I think I'll probably be the manager!

We sometimes argue but ⁷ none of us stays angry after a fight. We always say we're sorry because we think our friendship is more important than anything else.

Unit 15

1

you	you	yourself
he	him	himself
she	her	herself
it	it	itself
we	us	ourselves
you	you	yourselves
they	them	themselves

3
1 herself
2 yourselves
3 ourselves
4 himself
5 themselves
6 itself
7 yourself
8 herself
9 themselves
10 myself

4
1 by himself
2 by herself
3 by yourself
4 by yourelves
5 by ourselves
6 by myself
7 by himself
8 by myself

5
1 yourself
2 themselves
3 himself
4 herself
5 myself
6 yourself
7 myself

6
1 me
2 ourselves
3 herself
4 you
5 myself
6 himself
7 her

8 yourself
9 us
10 him

8
1 Peter and Lucy were shouting at each other.
2 They are looking at each other.
3 They don't talk to each other.
4 Erin and Vicky were looking at each other.
5 We trust each other.
6 Jenny and Lewis don't know each other.

9
1 each other
2 ourselves
3 himself
4 each other
5 yourselves
6 each other
7 each other
8 yourself

10
1 Be careful! You'll cut yourself!
2 I enjoy myself.
3 She'll watch it by herself.
4 Dad, have you / did you hurt yourself?
5 They must behave themselves.
6 Please, help yourself.

Unit 16

1

big	bigger than	the biggest
large	larger than	the largest
heavy	heavier than	the heaviest
expensive	more expensive than	the most expensive
slowly	more slowly than	the most slowly
fast	faster than	the fastest

3

old	older	oldest
easy	easier	easiest
important	more important	the most important
safe	safer	the safest
good	better	the best
funny	funnier	the funniest
difficult	more difficult	the most difficult
thin	thinner	the thinnest
bad	worse	the worst
popular	more popular	the most popular

4
1 deeper than
2 the longest
3 the largest

4 the highest
5 colder than
6 the biggest
7 longer than
8 higher than

6
1 quickly
2 hard
3 well
4 angrily
5 carefully
6 fast
7 badly
8 beautifully

7
1 busy
2 well
3 quietly
4 slow
5 bad
6 clearly
7 beautiful
8 safely

8
1 more carefully
2 harder
3 more regularly
4 more neatly
5 better
6 more seriously

10
1 isn't as big as
2 is as nice as
3 isn't as exciting as
4 isn't as good as
5 is as fast as
6 is as shy as
7 isn't as interesting as
8 is as easy as

11
1 as friendly as
2 as heavy as
3 as beautiful
4 as fast as
5 as interesting
6 as well as
7 difficult as
8 as intelligent as

13
1 I'm too tired to go out.
2 He was too angry to speak.

3   Ella was too excited to speak.
4   He works too slowly to finish the project by Monday.
5   Grandad's too old to play football with us.
6   Jenny's too busy to come with us.
7   You're too young to drive.
8   She plays too badly to be in our team.

14
1   He isn't tall enough to be a basketball player.
2   I'm not strong enough to move this table.
3   Lucy doesn't play the violin well enough to be a musician.
4   My bag isn't big enough to hold all these books.
5   Kevin isn't fit enough to be an athlete.
6   He doesn't run fast enough to win the race.
7   Amy didn't feel well enough to go to school.
8   They didn't work hard enough to pass the test.

15
1   Our living room isn't big enough to hold thirty people.
2   This bag isn't light enough to carry.
3   Dad felt too ill to go to work yesterday.
4   The documentary was too boring to watch.
5   It isn't warm enough to swim today.
6   The man was too angry to speak quietly.

16
1   the fastest
2   slower than
3   as tall as
4   as long as
5   well
6   as bad as

17
Students' own answers.

Unit 17

3
1	in	6	next
2	at	7	near
3	under	8	opposite
4	in front of	9	between
5	behind	10	in

4
1	at	5	At
2	on; at	6	On
3	On	7	At; in
4	In; in	8	on

6
1	along	5	down
2	out of	6	into
3	from; to	7	up
4	into	8	to

7
1	to	5	on
2	out of	6	in
3	in	7	at
4	next to	8	at

9
1	h	6	a
2	f	7	e
3	j8		i
4	g	9	b
5	c	10	d

10
1	about	6	for
2	at	7	to
3	about	8	about
4	for	9	to
5	to	10	for

11
1	of	6	in
2	with	7	on
3	with	8	of
4	for	9	about
5	of	10	at

12
1	in	6	on
2	to	7	for
3	at	8	at
4	about	9	to
5	at	10	at

13
1	b	6	c
2	c	7	b
3	a	8	a
4	c	9	b
5	a		

14
1	up	5	on
2	down	6	off
3	into	7	onto
4	out of	8	over

15
Students' own answers.

Use Your English 4

1
1	much	6	the
2	any	7	few
3	a	8	many
4	some	9	lot
5	no	10	little

2

1 quiet
2 are
3 the U.S.
4 fast
5 behind
6 yourselves
7 well
8 old enough
9 None
10 more slowly

3

1	at / by	5	How
2	for	6	in
3	one	7	the
4	than	8	nothing

4

1 as hard
2 badly
3 the tallest
4 tired to go
5 himself
6 each other

5

1	C	5	A
2	B	6	B
3	B	7	B
4	C	8	C

Unit 18

3

1 Katie wasn't at home ten minutes ago.
2 We met Irene in Germany last year.
3 He ate four sandwiches at school today!
4 Uncle Bob is picking us up from the airport in an hour.
5 I read a very interesting article in *Teenlink* last week.
6 We saw Tina at the supermarket on Monday.
7 I'm going to phone Amy at midday.
8 Mum and Dad were having tea in the garden at six.

4

1 I went to bed at ten o'clock.
2 We are going to meet Kelly outside the cinema at eight.
3 My cousins have been here since noon.
4 I found these old photos in the attic yesterday.
5 We didn't visit my grandparents last week.
6 I saw Emma and Sarah at school today.
7 Kim and I are playing tennis at the sports centre tomorrow.
8 Jim ate three pieces of cake at Mike's party on Saturday.

6

1 Becky will lend me her brown jacket.
2 She sent him a birthday card.
3 I'll show you my room.
4 The waiter brought us our food.
5 I'll give you some money.
6 He offered me some cake.

7

1 Lucy sent an email to Izumi.
2 Peter gave some flowers to Angela.
3 Beth lent her camera to Harry.
4 Harry wrote a letter to his cousin.
5 Lucy showed her new painting to Sophie.
6 Mrs Hardy offered some biscuits to Harry.

8

1 Kevin showed his new computer to Bob.
2 Anne sent her friend a postcard.
3 I won't give my email address to him.
4 Carol lent Suzie her laptop.
5 I wrote my brother a note.
6 Mrs Cooper offered some tea to her friend.
7 I'll give Sam your book.
8 Amy brought a CD to Lisa.

9 & 10
Students' own answers.

Unit 19

1

Do you like my new jacket?	Yes, I do.
Are you coming?	Yes, I am.
Was Ray at home?	No, he wasn't.
Did Lisa phone you last night?	Yes, she did.
Was your Mum working at eight?	Yes, she was.
Have you finished?	No, I haven't.
Had they gone to bed by six?	Yes, they had.
Are they going to stay at home?	No, they aren't.
Will you help us?	Yes, I will.
Should I talk to her about this?	Yes, you should.

3

1 Are; am
2 Has; hasn't
3 Were; was
4 Could; couldn't
5 Has; hasn't
6 Does; does
7 Did; did
8 Have; have
9 Was; was
10 Do; do

4
1 Did you go to bed early last night?
2 Are you wearing a T-shirt right now?
3 Have you ever met anyone famous?
4 Can your best friend speak German?
5 Were you watching TV at six yesterday?
6 Do you usually walk to school?
7 Is it raining right now?
8 Do you have to get up early tomorrow?
9 Are you going to stay at home on Saturday?
10 Does your best friend live in a flat?

5
1 Who's that boy over there?
2 Where did they go?
3 Whose bike is that?
4 Why is the baby crying?
5 How old is your sister?
6 How much did that T-shirt cost?
7 How many people were at the party?
8 How often do you see Kelly?

7
1 Where was Emma going?   e home.
2 What do you want for your   g A new
   birthday?   computer.
3 Which T-shirt should I buy?   a The blue one.
4 When did you buy this bike?   c Last year.
5 Whose camera did you borrow? h Mike's.
6 Who is that girl?   b That's Ella,
                                       Mrs Hastings'
                                       daughter.
7 Why did she leave so early?   f Because she
                                       was tired.
8 How often do you play football? d Every day.

8
1 How old is your sister?
2 What is she wearing?
3 When did you see her last?
4 Where was she?
5 What did she do after that?
6 How do you know that?
7 Why are you looking at me like that?

9 **Subject questions**
Who has invited you?

Object questions
Who did she call?
Who did Jim visit?
Who is she helping?

11
1 Who phoned her?
2 Who helped him?

3 Who broke the window?
4 Who took her keys?
5 Who saw us?
6 Who invited him?

12
1 can you see
2 has got your book
3 happened
4 did he buy
5 told Alex
6 is she trying to say
7 's coming
8 does he want

13
1 Who bought that painting?
2 What did she say?
3 Who found the money?
4 What was Sophie wearing?
5 Who's playing the violin?
6 Who did you phone?
7 Who won the game?
8 Who lives in that house?
9 What did Luke give you?
10 Who did you see?

14 Who's...
How old was...
Why is he wearing...
Who took
Where were...
Whose boat is it?
How many fish did you...

15
1 What did you have for breakfast this morning?
2 Who usually helps you with your homework?
3 Has your best friend ever been abroad?
4 What time do you usually get up on Sundays?
5 Who gave you the best present on your birthday?
6 How often do you go to the theatre?
7 Have you got any pets?
8 What is your favourite subject at school?
Students' own answers.

16
1 Who is your favourite actor?
2 Which sports do you like?
3 When did you decide to be a singer?
4 How often do you travel?
5 What is your star sign?
6 Do you have any brothers or sisters?

Unit 20

3
1 isn't she?
2 haven't you?
3 doesn't he?
4 aren't you?
5 isn't it?
6 isn't there?
7 aren't I?
8 won't you?

4
1 have you?
2 have we?
3 will you?
4 does she?
5 can they?
6 are you?
7 was she?
8 did he?

5
1 weren't you?
2 won't you?
3 do you?
4 didn't you?
5 is it?
6 haven't you?

8
1 Neither am I.
2 So did I.
3 Neither does mine.
4 So are we.
5 So was Jamie.
6 Neither did I.
7 So do I.
8 Neither have we.

9
1 b   6 a
2 a   7 b
3 c   8 a
4 c   9 c
5 a   10 b

10
1 You've got all your things, haven't you?
2 So do I.
3 Mum, you won't forget to buy biscuits, will you?
4 Neither do I.
5 You fed the cat, didn't you?
6 Let's watch the film, shall we?
7 So have I.

Unit 21

1
The rooms are cleaned every day.
The rooms were cleaned yesterday.

3
1 is made
2 are grown
3 is visited
4 am invited
5 is served
6 are fed
7 is taught
8 are painted

4
1 The toothbrush was invented in the fifteenth century.
2 The first pair of eyeglasses was worn in the 1200s.
3 The first bicycle was ridden in 1791.
4 The first hot dogs were eaten in the 1860s.
5 The first computer mouse was used in 1964.
6 The first CDs were sold in the 1980s.
7 The first public basketball game was played in 1892.

6
1 The invitation was sent to the wrong address.
2 is spoken
3 was stolen
4 are made
5 are wrapped
6 hotel was built
7 was sold
8 is thrown away

7
1 The exam papers are marked by Mrs Evans.
2 She was interviewed by a famous reporter.
3 Houses are designed by architects.
4 Coffee is grown in Brazil.
5 My new computer was delivered on Friday.
6 The window was broken by one of the students.
7 Her costume was designed by Jon Allan.
8 The treasure map was hidden in a secret place.

8
1 were inventd
2 was called
3 made
4 were made
5 is taken
6 reads
7 is given
8 help
9 is chosen
10 is added

11 is sent
12 is checked

9

1 Houses were heated
2 rooms were lit
3 milk was delivered by milkmen
4 it was stored
5 Food was cooked
6 Water was carried
7 clothes were washed
8 clothes were ironed
9 Irons were filled
10 Horse carriages were used

Use Your English 5

1

1 I saw Ben outside the supermarket yesterday.
2 He was waiting for his friend.
3 He is having a party for his birthday on Saturday.
4 He has invited all his friends from school.
5 Kelly is coming to the party, too.
6 Ben gave me her e-mail address.
7 I e-mailed her this morning.
8 Her mother is going to drive us to the party.
9 We are going to meet at her house at eight o'clock.
10 She is going to lend me her black skirt for the party.

2

1 Is this your first book?
2 How many books have you written?
3 When did you write your first book?
4 How old were you then?
5 Are you working on another book at the moment?
6 What's it about?
7 Could you sign this book for me, please?

3

1 were you?
2 shall we?
3 have you?
4 isn't she?
5 didn't they?
6 are they?
7 will you?
8 will he?

4

1 So do I.
2 Neither am I.
3 So did we.
4 Neither have I.
5 So can mine.
6 Neither does Alex.
7 So have we.
8 Neither did I.

5

1 are cleaned
2 was broken
3 was designed by
4 are made
5 were taken by
6 are written by
7 was sent
8 are marked by

6

1 's
2 was
3 did
4 to
5 have
6 do
7 So
8 you

Unit 22

1

Windsurfing is fun.
We went swimming yesterday.
I'm really bad at spelling.
I don't like drawing.

He came here to see you.
I don't want to try.
I'm sorry to hear about that.

3

1 Driving fast is dangerous.
2 Going out with friends is fun.
3 Travelling by plane is expensive.
4 Collecting stamps is interesting.
5 Eating sweets is bad for your teeth.
6 Playing golf is boring.
7 Walking is good exercise.
8 Smoking is bad for you.

4

1 Harry doesn't like skating.
2 Lucy is fond of painting.
3 Peter can't stand listening to Lucy's music.
4 My father often goes fishing.
5 I really enjoy cooking.
6 He is very keen on collecting model cars.
7 Chrissie never goes shopping at the weekends.
8 Kelly is afraid of walking in the dark.

6

1 to go
2 use
3 to help
4 to be
5 to drive
6 stay

7 to sell

8 cry

7

1 He came here to see you.

2 Amy went to the café to meet Katie.

3 They're going to Brighton to visit a friend.

4 Dad turned on the radio to listen to the news.

5 Kelly went out to buy a present for Tricia.

6 I phoned George to tell him about the party.

7 He stayed at home to finish his project.

8 I need a key to open that door.

8

1 to be

2 drawing

3 to see

4 swimming

5 wear

6 to help

7 watching

8 Using

9 reading

10 to visit

9

1 to do

2 to buy

3 to come

4 shopping

5 stay

6 to hear

7 bowling

8 go

9 bowling

10 to pay

10

Students' own answers.

Unit 23

1 Sophie says (that) she can make it shorter.
He wants to know what the article is about.

Sophie said that she could make it shorter.
He wanted to know what the article was about.

3

1 Holly says (that) she's thirteen years old.

2 She says (that) she lives in London.

3 She says (that) her parents work in a bank.

4 She says (that) she has got a twin sister.

5 She says (that) she loves pop music.

6 She says (that) she can speak German, French and Italian.

7 She says (that) she doesn't like science fiction films.

8 She says (that) her favourite subject is Art.

4

1 He wants to know what time the film starts.

2 He wants to know how much the ticket costs.

3 He wants to know if I can be ready at six.

4 He wants to know what time I have to be back.

5 He wants to know what I want to do after the film.

6 He wants to know if I want to go to the new fast food restaurant in West Street.

7 He wants to know if Val can come with us.

6

1 (that) he wanted to go home.

2 (that) she didn't like the food.

3 (that) we couldn't use his brother's computer.

4 (that) she had to be at the station at six.

5 (that) they were late.

6 (that) she didn't believe him.

7 (that) his sister worked in a bookshop.

8 (that) Anna wasn't at home.

7

1 who my best friend was.

2 what time I get up in the morning.

3 if my school was far.

4 if I like going to the cinema.

5 if I've got a TV in my room.

6 if I was tired.

7 if I could speak Spanish.

8 how much pocket money I get.

8

Suggested answer:

First, I asked Liam where he was from, and he said he was from Manchester.

Sophie asked him if he has got any brothers or sisters, and he said that he has one sister.

Sam asked what kind of music he liked, and he said (that) he loved pop music.

Dave asked Liam if he could play basketball, and he answered that he's very good at it.

Finally Laura asked if he liked our school, and Liam said it was great. He said everyone was very friendly.

Unit 24

1 That's the man who lives next door.
The car which is parked outside our house is Mr Taylor's.

This is the photo that was in the local newspaper.

The man whose car was stolen went to the police station.

3

1	who	6	which
2	which	7	who
3	who	8	which
4	which	9	which
5	who	10	who

4

1 who's
2 whose
3 who's
4 whose
5 who's
6 whose
7 who's
8 whose

5

1	it	5	they
2	them	6	it
3	she	7	it
4	he	8	she

6

1 A reporter is someone who works for a newspaper.
2 An author is someone who writes books.
3 A parrot is a bird that can talk.
4 A ruler is something (that) we use to draw straight lines.
5 A dentist is someone who / that looks after your teeth.
6 A waiter is someone who / that works in a restaurant.
7 An ostrich is a very large bird that can run very fast.
8 A thief is a person who / that steals things.

7

1 There's the house (that) my aunt wants to buy.
2 An old man, who was Jake's Grandfather, opened the door.
3 *Wanted* is the film that / which made him famous.
4 The girl (who is) standing over there is my cousin.
5 That's the boy whose mother teaches English at our school.
6 Here's the note (that) Ben left for you this morning.
7 I ate the sandwich that was in the fridge.
8 We stayed in a hotel which / that had a huge swimming pool.

8

1	b	5	a
2	a	6	c
3	c	7	a
4	b		

9

1 A thief who stole a car from a supermarket car park jumped out of it only minutes later.
2 A dog that / which had been asleep on the back seat woke up.
3 He was looking for a car that / which was unlocked.
4 He did not see the great dane that / which was asleep on the back seat.
5 He saw the dog that / which was making the growling noise.
6 A woman who was walking home from the supermarket saw the thief running away.

Unit 25

1 She phoned David and told him about the party.

She phoned David but she didn't tell him about the party.

I stayed at home because I was tired.

I was tired, so I stayed at home.

She bought the dress although it was very expensive.

3

1 and
2 and
3 but
4 and
5 but
6 but
7 and
8 but

4

1 because
2 so
3 because
4 because
5 so
6 because
7 so
8 so

5

1 We can't go to the concert because we've lost the tickets.
2 She was late so she took a taxi.
3 I couldn't get up in the morning because I went to bed late last night.
4 She was asleep so she didn't hear the bell.
5 Mum didn't let me go to the cinema because I hadn't tidied my room.
6 Jamie had eaten too much ice cream so he had a stomachache.
7 I didn't have enough money, so I didn't buy that book.
8 He's hungry because he didn't have breakfast.

6
1 Although it was raining, we went out. / We went out although it was raining.
2 Although I hate horror films, I liked this one.
3 Although Tim is only eight, he can speak three languages. / Tim ca speak three languages although he's only eight.
4 He was wearing a jacket although it was hot.
5 I couldn't sleep although I was tired. / Although I was tired, I couldn't sleep.
6 Although I got up late, I arrived on time. / I arrived on time although I got up late.
7 Although Becky worked hard, she didn't pass the test. / Becky didn't pass the test although she worked hard.
8 They're twins, although they're quite different. / Although they're quite different, they're twins.

7
1 and   5 but
2 but   6 and
3 so   7 so
4 and   8 although

8
1 c   4 a
2 a   5 b
3 b   6 c

9
Suggested answers:

Hi, Lucy!

I've got great news![1] Dad's got some business in London next week and he's promised to take me with him! [2] Mum isn't very happy because I'll miss school for three days. [3] I'll have to work harder when we come back but I don't mind. [4] It will be great to see you and spend some time with you! I've missed you!

XXX

Lisa

Hi, cousin!

I've missed you, too! [5] Although I have to go to school on weekdays, I'm already planning what we're going to do at the weekend! [6] First of all, it's Dad's birthday on Friday, so we're all going out for a family meal. [7] On Saturday morning, I usually go skating in the park but we could do something else if you're not into it. In the afternoon, Beth's invited a few friends to her house. [8] I've told her all about you and she's dying to meet you. [9] I've left Sunday free because we're going to do anything you like!

Love,

Lucy

Use Your English 6

1
1 playing
2 painting
3 stay
4 to go
5 to visit
6 listening
7 cry
8 walking

2
1 (that) she had to get up early on Saturday.
2 if I could get some ice cream for the party.
3 (that) she could buy the food and soft drinks.
4 (that) she wanted some balloons, too.
5 how many CDs I could bring.
6 she didn't want to wear her red dress.
7 (that) she hated it.
8 if she could borrow my black skirt.

3
1 The man who's standing next to Anna is her uncle.
2 Mike took the money which was on the table.
3 That's the boy whose dog bit me!
4 They've got a cat which sleeps in our garden all the time.
5 Penguins are birds which can't fly.
6 I met a girl whose father is a famous author.
7 That's the man who stole my bag!
8 They bought a flat which is much bigger than ours.

4
1 so
2 and
3 but
4 so
5 but
6 so
7 because

5
1 B
2 C
3 A
4 A
5 C
6 B
7 B
8 C

Teacher's notes for photocopiable activity sheets

Teacher's notes for photocopiable activity sheets

Unit 1

Preparation: Photocopy one activity sheet for each pair of pupils. Cut each sheet in half along the dotted line. Give one sheet A and one sheet B to each pair.

1 Ask and answer to find out about Jack. Use the present simple or present continuous.

- Explain that pupils take turns to ask questions and fill in the missing information on their sheets.
- Point out the first prompts in the texts and write the example questions on the board:
  A: *Where does Jack work?*
  B: *Where does Jack live?*
- Ask the pupils to find the answers in their texts.
- Pupils work in pairs and take turns to ask each other questions and complete the sentences on their sheets.
- Go through the answers with the class, writing up the complete text on the board.

Answers

A	B
1 works at the Mango restaurant	1 in a small flat
2 9 o'clock	2 at 11.30 a.m.
3 plays tennis	3 he goes swimming
4 staying at his flat	4 shopping in town
5 some new clothes	5 cooking a meal
6 an apple cake	6 eats at the restaurant

Unit 2

Preparation: Photocopy one activity sheet for every pupil in the class.

1 Read, and complete.

- Explain that pupils need to fill in the verbs in the past simple to complete the story about a robbery that happened last week.
- Focus pupils on the first sentence and read the

beginning of the story with the class. Ask them to give the correct form of '*buy*' for number 2.

- Pupils work on their own to complete the story.

Answers

1	went	10	ran
2	bought	11	tried
3	had	12	shouted
4	watched	13	jumped
5	cried	14	dropped
6	Did you like	15	Did you study
7	asked	16	were
8	nodded	17	was
9	walked		

2 Take turns to ask and answer questions with your partner.

- Divide the class into pairs.
- Explain that pupils are going to take turns to ask and answer the questions about the robbery. Tell them that they will have to be detectives and check the story to find the answers.

Answers

1 They went to the cinema.
2 No, she bought a drink.
3 A love story.
4 Yes, she did.
5 After the film.
6 He tried to take Hannah's mobile phone.
7 No, an old woman stopped the man.
8 No. She used to be a police officer.

Unit 3

Preparation: Photocopy one activity sheet for each pupil.

- Explain that pupils have to make as many sentences with *when* as possible, using the words in the grid.
- Demonstrate the activity. Ask pupils to help you make a sentence using the past continuous and past simple, eg: *He was having a bath when the dog jumped in.* Write the sentence on the board. Make another sentence together if necessary.
- Pupils work in pairs/groups to continue making sentences following the example.

Possible Answers

He was having a bath when the dog jumped in.
We were climbing the tree when Jack fell out.
They were listening to the band when it started to rain.
They were swimming when they saw a shark.
She was driving when a ball hit the car.
He was running to the shop when he fell over.
She was tidying her room when she broke the TV.
We were playing in the park when we saw an elephant.

- When they have finished, ask the pupils to write their sentences in their notebooks. The pair/group to make the most correct sentences is the winner.

Unit 4

Preparation: Photocopy one activity sheet for every pupil in the class.

1 Listen, read and tick the correct box.

- Explain that you are going to tell the pupils about a racing driver. Read the text out once.
- Now ask the pupils to look at the questions on their sheets. Explain that you are going to read the text again and they should listen and answer the questions by ticking the *yes* or *no* boxes.

Script

Hi! My name's Paul Davies and I'm a racing driver. I love my job! I've driven in over fifty races in Europe and I've never had an accident. I have also been to China, Mexico and America, but I haven't visited Canada.

The next race is in Paris. I've been there four times. It's a great city! My new car is French. It's got a huge engine and it's the fastest car I have ever driven.

My mum and dad have moved from England to France. They have watched most of my races. Today I took the new car for a test drive. Dad doesn't like fast cars so he's never been on a test drive.

Answers

1	Yes	3	No	5	Yes	7	No
2	Yes	4	No	6	No		

2 Ask your partner. Use the words to help you.

- Use the example and first prompt to demonstrate the activity. Then ask the pupils to work in pairs and take turns to ask and answer questions.

Unit 5

Preparation: Photocopy one activity sheet for every pupil in the class.

1 Unjumble the sentences.

- Pupils look at the words for the first sentence. Ask pupils to make a sentence by putting the words in the correct order.
- Ask pupils to work on their own and order the words for the other sentences.

Answers

1 Mary has been a doctor since 2004.
2 We have already bought the apples and cola.
3 Harry hasn't read the comic yet.
4 My parents have been on holiday for two weeks.
5 My cat hasn't caught a mouse yet.
6 Kate has already left the gym.
7 Steve has just painted the chair.
8 My friends have been chefs for ten years.

2 True/False sentences.

- Demonstrate the exercise, using the first sentence as an example. Point out that pupils need to use their sentences from part 1 to decide whether the answer is true or false.

Answers

1	T	3	F	5	T	7	F
2	F	4	T	6	F	8	T

3 Play the True/False game

- Pupils work individually to write the sentences. Remind them that one of their sentences should be false.
- Ask one pupil to read their sentences aloud to the class. Ask the class to guess which sentence is not true.
- Divide the pupils into pairs to take turns reading their sentences. Their partner guesses which sentence is false.

Unit 6

Preparation: Photocopy one activity sheet for every pupil in the class.

1 Read, choose and complete.

- Pupils complete the sentences using the words in the box.

Answers

1	already	4	By	7	because
2	When	5	had	8	hadn't
3	just	6	before	9	by

2 Look at exercise 1 again. Write three questions. Ask your partner.

- Go through the example questions. Ask pupils to look at exercise 1 and find the sentence about Jake. Ask: *What had Jake's friends done?* and write the question on the board. Prompt the answer: *They had finished their lunch.* Repeat with sentence 4 about James.
- Pupils choose three sentences from exercise 1 and write questions. When they have finished, they can ask their partner the questions.

3 Choose and write the best ending for each sentence.

- Pupils should read each sentence opening, then choose the best ending from the list to complete the sentence.

Answers

1 f 2 e 3 g 4 c 5 d 6 b 7 a

Unit 7

Preparation: Photocopy one activity sheet for every pupil in the class.

1 Write a sentence in each box. Use capital letters.

- Write the headings from the three boxes on the board. Ask pupils what they might do after school. Write one of the ideas under the first heading using the present continuous, eg:

After school
I'm playing tennis.

- Repeat with the other two headings. Use the future *going to* for **Next summer**, eg *I'm*

going to stay with my best friend, and *will* for **When I'm 20**, eg *I think I'll open a zoo.*

- Pupils write a sentence in each box about themselves. They should write in capital letters using blue ink so that individual handwriting is less recognisable.

2 Cut the sentences out. Play the guessing game in a group of four.

- Ask the pupils to cut out the three sentence boxes from exercise 1. Then organise the class into groups of four and get them to collect the group's sentences, shuffle them and place them face down in the middle.
- Demonstrate the game. Take the top card from one group's pile and try to guess who wrote it. Say, eg: *Sam will open a zoo.* Sam then says whether this is true or not, eg: *Yes, I will open a zoo* or *No, I won't open a zoo.* Explain that if the player has guessed correctly, they keep the question. If not, they put it at the bottom of the pile. If a pupil picks up one of their own statements they should put it on the bottom of the pile and take another card.
- The pupils play the game. The pupil with the most questions at the end is the winner.

Unit 8

Preparation: Photocopy one activity sheet for each pair of pupils.

1 Read and write.

- Explain that pupils are going to write their own set of rules for visitors to a fairground they have just opened. Write the modal verbs from the activity sheets on the board. Brainstorm a few example sentences with the class and write them on the board if necessary, eg *You can have lunch in the cafe, You mustn't jump off the rides.* Encourage pupils to make both negative and positive sentences.
- Pupils work in pairs to produce eight rules for visitors.

2 Vote for the best rules.

- Pupils read their rules out. The class votes for the best rule made up by each pair.
- They can then make a final version of the best rules for a class display.

Unit 9

Preparation: Photocopy one activity sheet for every pupil in the class

1 Match.

- Use the example to show pupils how to match the parts of the sentences. Pupils complete the activity on their own.
- Pupils should work in pencil so they can correct mistakes.

Answers
1 You should bring a camera.
2 Take a drink because you might get thirsty.
3 You shouldn't run across the road.
4 We could go swimming after lunch.
5 It's raining so I may not go to the park.
6 You can't be cold because it's a hot day.
7 I may stay in bed as I don't feel well.

2 Write the sentences. Underline the modal verbs.

- Pupils write out the sentences from exercise 1 in full, then circle the modal verbs.

Answers:
1 You (should) bring a camera.
2 Take a drink because you (might) get thirsty.
3 You (shouldn't) run across the road
4 We (could) go swimming after lunch.
5 It's raining so I (may) not go to the park.
6 You (can't) be cold because it's a very hot day.
7 I (may) stay in bed as I don't feel well.

3 Work with a partner. Read and talk about what to do. Use the words in bold in your responses.

- Read the first prompt with the class. Point out the words in bold (**should/shouldn't**) and ask volunteers to think of response using *should*. Repeat with *shouldn't*.
- Divide the class into pairs and ask them to think of as many sensible responses as they can to the prompts. Circulate, checking the pupils are using the correct key words in their responses.
- Now write sentences.
- Pupils should work on their own to choose and write the best response to each prompt.

Suggested answers
1 You should stay at home. / You should take some medicine.
2 They might be at work / the theatre.
3 We could go to the beach if it's sunny. / We could go to the cinema if it rains.
4 He must be exhausted. / He must be very thirsty.

Unit 10

Preparation: Photocopy one activity sheet for every pupil in the class.

1 Write *offer* or *suggestion* after each sentence.

- Pupils read each sentence and decide if it is an offer or suggestion. If you think it necessary, go through the first example with the class.
- Pupils work on their own to complete the activity by writing the correct function at the end of each sentence.

Answers
1 offer	3 suggestion	5 suggestion
2 suggestion	4 offer	6 offer

2 Write.

- Pupils take turns to make the offers and suggestions from exercise 1. They should tick the ideas for activities they both agree on.

3 Talk to your partner. Use the phrases to help you answer.

- Explain that pupils should take turns to make the offers and suggestions from exercise 2.
- They should use the prompts to help them answer their partner's questions. Demonstrate this by asking a pupil to make a suggestion and then respond yourself using one of the prompts.
- When they have finished they should tick the ideas for activities they both agree on.

4 Agree to do three things. Tell the class.

- Pupils decide which three things they would like to do most. They then report back their preferences to the class.

Unit 11

Preparation: Photocopy one activity sheet for every pupil in the class.

1 Match and write sentences.

- Explain that the pupils need to find and make seven sentences. Write the first part of the example conditional sentence on the board Ask pupils to find the second part of the sentence. Write this on the board and let pupils complete it on their sheets.
- Pupils work on their own to complete the remaining conditional sentences.

Answers

If I eat cheese, / I feel sick.
He'll go to university / if he passes his exams.
If I found £50, / I'd buy a new dress.
If you see Becky, / ask her to phone me.
I wouldn't eat so much / if I were you.
We'll miss the show / if we don't leave now.
When it's sunny, / I am happy.

2 Write three wishes.

- Go through the example with the class. Then ask them to talk about their wishes, prompting ideas if necessary, eg *didn't have to go to school/ could draw well*, etc. Write key words on the board.
- Pupils work on their own write down their three wishes.

3 Now write what you would do if your wishes came true.

- Pupils write a conditional sentence for each wish. Encourage them to read their wishes and conditional sentences to the class.

Unit 12

Preparation: Photocopy one activity sheet for every pupil in the class.

1 Look and complete the sentences.

- Explain that the pupils are going to use the picture prompts to complete their sentences. Go through the example with the class, pointing out that they need to use the plural form of *pizza* in the sentence.
- The pupils complete the remaining sentences. They can either work on their own or in pairs.

Answers

1 There are three pizzas in the fridge.
2 The leaves are falling off the trees now.
3 They have both got very short spiky hair.
4 Both these pairs of jeans are great!
5 How many tomatoes have we got?
6 Look! There are lots of fish in the river.
7 We need to buy some more cherries.
8 I can see two men taking the furniture to the van.

2 Read and complete with *a/an* or *the*.

- Pupils read and complete the text using *a, an* or *the*.

Answers

1 an	3 a	5 a	7 a
2 an	4 an	6 the	8 the

Unit 13

Preparation: Photocopy one activity sheet for each pair of pupils. Cut each sheet in half along the dotted line. Give one sheet A and one sheet B to each pair.

1 Read the instructions and complete the table for yourself.

- Go through the instructions with the class and make sure they understand that they must answer truthfully about what the have to eat and drink in a day.
- Pupils work on their own to complete the table about themselves using ticks and crosses. They should use the *Me* column for this part of the exercise.

2 Now ask your partner.

- Demonstrate this activity with a pupil. Write on the board: *How much fruit do you eat?* And *How many glasses of water do you drink*? Add a heading *My Partner*. Ask the first question, and elicit the answer. Fill in the column appropriately. Repeat with the second question.
- Pupils work in pairs to ask and answer questions and complete their tables.

3 Write about your partner.

- Pupils work on their own to write about their partner following the model given.
- Ask some of the pupils to read their texts to the class.

Unit 14

Preparation: Photocopy one activity sheet for every three pupils in the class.

- Divide the class into groups of three and give each group an activity sheet. The pupils cut the cue cards out and place them in a pile face down.
- Demonstrate the activity by turning over a card. Write the cues (shown below) for the appropriate card on the board. Prompt pupils to make a sentence beginning *Both* or *All*, eg for *ostrich* and *penguin*: *Both of them are birds,* for *Australia, Egypt, Canada: All of them are countries* Then ask them to make a second sentence beginning *Neither* or *None*, eg: *Neither of them can fly. / None of them are in Europe.*

Cues:

birds / fly   actors / Spanish   wheels / windows
sports / team games
Months / winter   wild animals / pets
countries / Europe   tails / hands
swim / walk   tall / red   cities / America
drinks / cold

- Explain that pupils will play a game in their groups using the cards. They must turn over a card and make two sentences. If they can do this successfully they keep their card, if not they should place it at the bottom of the pile. The winner is the pupil with the most cards at the end.
- Then ask pupils to turn all the cards face up. They should choose two or three cards. Pupils write two new sentences for each card in their notebooks.

Unit 15

Preparation: Photocopy one activity sheet for every pupil in the class.

1 Find and write the questions.

- Go through the example with the class, making sure they check that the question couldn't go with any of the other answers.
- Pupils work on their own to find and write the questions in the correct place.

2 Circle the best answer.

- Pupils circle the correct word in each answer.

Answers
1 What happened?
  She went to the hospital by herself.
2 What are they doing?
  They're testing each other.
3 Can I help you?
  No, it's okay. We'll do it ourselves.
4 Where are you going Jack?
  I'm going for a walk by myself.
5 Did Gerry have guitar lessons?
  No, he taught himself.
6 Did they have fun at the water park?
  Yes, they really enjoyed themselves.
7 Shall I turn the cooker off?
  It's okay, it will go off by itself.

3 Write three questions for your partner to answer.

- Pupils use the questions and answers from exercises 1 and 2 to help them write their own similar questions. They then ask their partner the questions. Make sure the pupils are using reflexive pronouns or *each other* in their answers.

Unit 16

Preparation: Photocopy one activity sheet for every pupil in the class.

1 Read and complete.

- Explain that Ella has written a letter to her friend, Becky. Ask pupils to complete the letter by putting the missing words in the correct place.

Answers
1 older	4 harder	7 carefully
2 better	5 easiest	8 good
3 worst	6 seriously	9 fastest

2 Answer the questions.

- Pupils read the completed letter in exercise 1 and answer the questions. They should use one word answers.

Answers
| 1 her brother | 3 English | 5 Denise |
| 2 Maths | 4 Angie | |

3 **Write three questions for your partner to answer.**

- Pupils write three more questions. Then they can either ask their partner the questions or swap papers and write the answers to their partner's questions.

Unit 17

Preparation: Photocopy one activity sheet for every three pupils in the class.

- Divide the class into groups of three. Give one activity sheet to each group. Ask them to cut the sheets into three along the dotted lines and share the sheets out.
- Explain that they are going to play a game. Pupils take turns to choose a preposition from the box on the left and a word cue from the box on the right. Then they make a sentence using these words, eg: *I'm afraid of vampires / Peter ran round the corner*. If the others in the group agree that the sentence is grammatically correct, they can tick off the words they have used. If not, they can try again with these words on their next turn, or they can choose two new words. The winner is the first person to tick all the words on their cards.
- Pupils play the game in their groups. Check they are playing the game correctly and help with any difficulties they may have.

Unit 18

Preparation: Photocopy one activity sheet for every pupil in the class.

1 **Write sentences.**

- Pupils put the words in order and write sentences. Make sure they remember to use capital letters and full stops.

Answers
1 They were laughing at the clown.
2 He forgot to get some bread.
3 We are going to the concert after lunch.
4 She bought Jack some magazines.
5 They showed me their new house.
6 I'm going on holiday next week.
7 I lent my best dress to Julie.
8 We are playing basketball at 3 o'clock.

2 **Take turns with your partner to make sentences.**

- Write the example prompt (*is playing*) and sentence (*Lucy is playing tennis*) on the board. Ask the class to make a longer sentence, eg: *Lucy is playing tennis at 4 o'clock*. If pupils have difficulty, tell them to think about time and place.
- Pupils work in pairs. Explain that they should each choose one prompt and write the first sentence. Then they swap work sheets and expand their partner's first sentence. They should continue this way until they have completed all four sentences.

3 **Now write your own sentences.**

- Pupils write their own set of sentences from the prompt they didn't use in exercise 2.

Unit 19

Preparation: Photocopy one activity sheet for every pupil in the class.

1 **Complete each question. Find and write the answer.**

- Explain that pupils are going to complete a conversation between Chloe and her friend Beth.
- Go through the example question and answer with the class. Explain that pupils should find each answer as they write the question.
- Pupils work on their own to complete the dialogue.

Answers
1 Did you have a great birthday?
  Yes, I did.
2 Which present did you like most?
  The tickets for a concert.
3 Who gave you the tickets?
  Mum and dad.
4 Who did you see at the concert?
  Duffy - she's a great singer.
5 Where was the concert?
  In London.
6 How did you get there?
  By train.
7 Who did you go with?
  I went with Mum and Hannah.
8 Was it a good concert?
  Yes, it was brilliant!

9 How many people were there?
Over 20,000.
10 Did your mum like Duffy?
No, she didn't.

2 **Ask your partner questions about their birthday. Use the questions in exercise 1 to help you.**

- Explain that pupils are going to ask a partner about their last birthday. Get them to read out some of the question forms from exercise 1. As they do this, write question prompts on the board, eg: *What…?*, etc. Then ask if they can think of any more questions they could ask and add these new prompts.
- Pupils work in pairs to ask and answer questions. They should try to use as many question forms as they can.
- Circulate and help any pairs who are having problems formulating accurate questions or answers. They should swap roles after five questions have been asked.

Unit 20

Preparation: Photocopy one activity sheet for every pupil in the class.

1 **Rewrite the sentences adding question tags.**

- Go through the example with the class. Explain that pupils need to rewrite each sentence adding the appropriate question tag.
- Circulate as the pupils work, and ensure they are using the correct question tags.
- If you have time, invite pupils to come and write their new sentences on the board.

Answers
1 You're from Italy, aren't you?
2 Sally can't drive, can she?
3 They didn't go to the art class today, did they?
4 Let's watch the game, shall we?
5 I'm good at making cakes, aren't I?
6 He's got brown hair, hasn't he?
7 Stop playing that music, will you?
8 Mum's going to buy a new TV, isn't she?
9 Eating lots of fruit is good for you, isn't it?

2 **Work with a partner. Take turns to agree with the statements.**

- Write the example statement on the board. Ask the class to read it aloud. Then ask them to agree with the statement, prompting them to look at the example if necessary. Write this on the board.
- Pupils work in pairs. They take turns to make and agree with the statements.

Answers
I'm going to learn to ski.	So am I.
I've got a lot of CDs.	So have I.
I didn't go shopping yesterday.	
Neither/Nor did I.	
I went on holiday last summer.	So did I.
I haven't finished my homework yet.	
Neither/Nor have I.	
I want some chocolate.	So do I.
My dad doesn't play any instruments.	
Neither/Nor do I.	

- If there is time, start a chain game around the class. One pupil makes a statement, the person nearest them agrees with it. This pupil makes the next statement, and so on. Encourage pupils to make up new statements, but if anyone gets stuck they can choose one from their worksheet.

Unit 21

Preparation: Photocopy one activity sheet for every pupil in the class.

1 **Work with your partner. Match and complete the sentences.**

- Go through the example (*The Eiffel Tower was built in 1889*) with the class, asking a pupil to underline the verb. Ensure pupils understand they need to produce the correct form of the verb shown in brackets on their activity sheets. Point out that these verbs will help them find the correct matching part of the sentence.
- Pupils work in pairs to match and complete the sentences.

Answers
1 The Eiffel Tower was built in 1889.
2 Yoghurt is made from milk.
3 Over 60 languages are spoken in Mexico.
4 Paper was invented about 2000 years ago.

5 *Sunflowers* and *Starry Night* were painted by Van Gogh.
6 100 iPods are sold every minute.
7 *Macbeth* was written by Shakespeare.
8 Fruit and vegetables are grown by farmers.

2 Write the sentences in full.

- Pupils work on their own to write the sentences from exercise 1 in full.

3 Write four more sentences using the prompts.

- Begin by getting the class to brainstorm sentences using one of the given verbs, eg: *The telephone was invented by Graham Bell.*
- Pupils write four new sentences. Encourage them to use the sentences in Exercise 2 as a model for their own work.

Unit 22

Preparation: Photocopy one activity sheet for each pair of pupils.

1 Work with a partner. Take turns to rewrite the sentences.

- Focus on the example. Show pupils how the first part of the sentence: *Snowboarding* is *great* is changed to make the new sentence: *Skiing* is *great*. Ask pupils to tell you what part of the third sentence has changed. Point out that the separated tint boxes indicate where they should split the sentence.
- Write the first sentence on the board and encourage pupils to think of another way of changing the first part of this sentence, eg: *Swimming* is *great*. Repeat with the second part of the sentence.
- Pupils work in pairs and take turns to modify each sentence. Encourage pupils to check their partner's sentences before they write a new one. They should work in pencil so they can correct mistakes.

2 Rewrite this sentence as many times as you can.

- Pupils work on their own to make new sentences as before. Give the pupils three minutes to make as many sentences as they can.
- If you have time, ask pupils to take turns to write their sentences on the board. They

should do this following the pattern of only changing one part of the sentence at a time. See how long the class can make the sentence chain.

Unit 23

Preparation: Photocopy one activity sheet for every pupil in the class.

1 Report what the speakers say.

- Pupils rewrite the direct speech in the speech bubbles as reported speech. Work through the example with the class. Point out that pupils need to use the present tense in their reported sentences.
- Pupils work on their own and write their sentences under the speech bubbles.

Answers
1 He says he wants to go to the party.
2 She says she has got to do lots of homework.
3 She says she loves apple pie.
4 He says he can't run very fast.
5 She says she is hungry and thirsty.
6 She says her sister lives in Spain.

2 Write a report of the conversation.

- Begin by asking two pupils to the front. Ask them to act out the dialogue between the policeman and the boy for the class.
- Focus on the first two sentences in the handwritten report. Tell pupils to check the dialogue and find the first question the policeman asked. Ask a volunteer to change the direct question into a reported question, prompting them to use the past tense if necessary. Explain that pupils should do this for the rest of the dialogue.
- Pupils can either work on their own or in pairs to complete their reports.

Answers
The policeman asked Billy where his parents were.
Billy said they were at home.
The policeman wanted to know what time Billy had to go home.
Billy said he had to be at home by 9 o'clock.
The policeman asked/wanted to know what was in Billy's bag.
Billy said it was a duck.

The policeman said Billy/he couldn't carry a duck in a bag.
Billy said it was okay – it was a toy duck.

Unit 24

Preparation: Photocopy one activity sheet for every pupil in the class.

1 Complete the puzzles. Write the missing name and *who, which, that* or *whose*.

- The pupils read and complete the descriptions with the appropriate relative pronoun and missing name.
- If you have enough time, invite pupils to write their completed descriptions on the board.

Answers
1 An **umbrella** is something **which / that** we can use in the rain.
2 A **baker** is a person **who / that** works in a bakery.
3 A **giraffe** is an animal **whose** neck is very long.
4 A **vet** is a person **who / that** looks after sick animals.
5 A **butcher's** is a shop **which / that** sells meat.
6 A **butterfly** is an insect **whose** wings have bright colours.

2 Finish the sentences.

- Pupils complete the sentences using their own words for the definitions. Demonstrate this by writing the example on the board and asking pupils to think of other ways to finish the same sentence, eg: *A cat is a furry animal which / that drinks milk*. Remind pupils they can use *which* when talking about things and animals, and *that* for people, things or animals.
- Pupils complete the sentences. When they have finished, ask pupils to read out their definitions.

Possible answers
1 A cat is a small animal which / that likes to chase mice.
2 A glass is something which / that we use to drink from.
3 A nurse is a person who / that looks after sick people in hospital.

4 A ball is a round toy which / that people use to play football.
5 An Italian is a person who / that comes from Italy.
6 A lion is a wild animal which / that lives in Africa.

3 Write four more sentence openers.

- Pupils write four more sentence openers like those in exercise 2. They should be about people, animals and things.

4 Ask your partner to complete the sentences.

- Pupils swap activity sheets and complete the definitions started by their partner. Encourage pupils to use all the relative pronouns they know.

Unit 25

Preparation: Photocopy one activity sheet for every pupil in the class.

1 Choose subjects from Box A and write sentences using linking words from Box B.

- Write the example sentence on the board and ask a pupil to come and underline the linking word. Choose a new linking word from Box B and write it on the board. Ask pupils to think of another sentence about the same subject but using the new linking work.
- Pupils write their own sentences choosing five subjects from Box A and using each of the linking words in Box B.

2 Write your own story. Use all the linking words from Box B in exercise 1.

- Explain that pupils are going to write their own story. They can write about whatever they want, but they must use all the linking words from Box B in exercise 1 in their story.
- If pupils need help getting started with their stories, brainstorm some ideas for titles with the class, eg *Last summer, My holiday, An accident*, and write them on the board. Pupils then write their own stories.
- Circulate and help pupils who have any difficulties with vocabulary, etc.

Unit 1

A

1 **Ask and answer to find out about Jack. Use the present simple or present continuous.**

> **A**: Where does Jack work?

> **B**: He works at the Mango restaurant

Jack is a waiter. He (*Where/work?*) ¹ _works at the Mango Restaurant_ in Brighton. He lives in a small flat near the restaurant.

On work days Jack gets up at (*What time?*) ² .... in the morning. He starts work at 11.30 and finishes very late in the evening.

On Saturdays Jack always (*What/do?*) ³ .... at the Sports Centre. On Sunday afternoons he goes swimming.

This weekend Jack's friends are (*Where/stay?*) ⁴ .... Right now they are shopping in town. They're buying (*What/buy?*) ⁵ ....

Jack is cooking a meal at the moment. He's trying to make (*What/make?*) ⁶ .... He doesn't often cook at home. He usually eats at the restaurant.

✂ ....

B

1 **Ask and answer to find out about Jack. Use the present simple or present continuous.**

> **B**: Where does Jack live?

> **A**: He lives in a small flat near the restaurant

Jack is a waiter. He works at the Mango Restaurant in Brighton. He lives (*Where/live?*) ¹ _in a small flat_ near the restaurant.

On work days Jack gets up at 9 o'clock in the morning. He starts work (*What time?*) ² .... and finishes very late in the evening.

On Saturdays Jack always plays tennis at the Sports Centre. On Sunday afternoons (*What/do?*) ³ ....

This weekend Jack's friends are staying at his flat. Right now they are (*What/do?*) ⁴ .... They're buying some new clothes.

Jack is (*What/do?*) ⁵ .... at the moment. He's trying to make an apple cake. He doesn't often cook at home. He usually (*Where/eat?*) ⁶ ....

Unit 2

1 **Complete the story. Put the verbs in brackets into the correct form.**

Last Wednesday Hannah [1] ....*went*........................... (go) to the cinema with Susie.
Hannah [2] .... (buy) an ice-cream and Susie
[3] .... (have) a drink.

They [4] .... (watch) a love story and Susie
[5] .... (cry) at the end.

[6] " .... (you/like) the film?"
[7] .... (ask) Hannah. Susie
[8] .... (nod).

After the film they [9] .... (walk) to the bus stop. A man
[10] .... (run) over and [11] ....
(try) to take Hannah's mobile phone.

"Stop that man," she [12] .... (shout). "He's got my phone."

An old woman [13] .... (jump) on the man and he
[14] .... (drop) the phone.

"Thank you," said Hannah. "[15] .... (you/study) judo when
you [16] .... (be) young?"

"No," said the woman. "But I [17] .... (be) a police officer."

2 **Take turns to ask and answer the questions with your partner.**

1 Where did Hannah and Susie go last week?
 They went to the cinema. ....

2 Did Susie buy an ice-cream? ....

3 What film did the girls watch? ....

4 Did Susie like the film? ....

5 When did the girls arrive at the bus-stop? ....

6 What did the man do? ....

7 Did the girls stop the man? ....

8 Did the woman study judo? ....

Unit 3

1 **Make sentences. Use the words in the chart below.**

he	ball	a dog	break the TV
they	tidy her room	she	fall over
band	swim	we	play in the park
drive	to the shop	see	listen to
climb a tree	start	an elephant	have a bath
rain	see	fall out	jump in
run	a shark	hit	the car

They were swimming in the sea when they saw a shark.

Unit 4

1 **Listen, read and tick the correct box.**

	Yes	No
1 Has Paul driven in over fifty races?	☐	☐
2 Has he ever raced in Europe?	☐	☐
3 Has Paul ever had an accident?	☐	☐
4 Has he been to Canada?	☐	☐
5 Have Paul's parents moved to France?	☐	☐
6 Have they watched all his races?	☐	☐
7 Has Paul's father ever been on a test drive?	☐	☐

2 **Ask and answer. Use the prompts below.**

A: Have you ever had an accident?   **B:** Yes, I have.

have / accident

climb / mountain

go / Canada

use / video camera

eat at / Chinese restaurant

see / pyramids

drive / car

make / meal

Unit 5

1   Put these sentences into the correct order.

1 has since Mary 2004 a been doctor
   Mary has been a doctor since 2004
....

2 bought we and apples have already the cola
....

3 yet Harry read hasn't comic the
....

4 parents on weeks my have for been two holiday
....

5 hasn't yet cat the my mouse caught
....

6 already left Kate gym has the
....

7 painted just has chair the Steve
....

8 friends ten chefs my been for have years
....

2   Are these sentences true (T) or false (F)?

1 Mary was a doctor in 2005. ☐
2 There is cola in our shopping basket, but there aren't any apples. ☐
3 Harry has already read the comic. ☐
4 My parents were on holiday a week ago. ☐
5 The cat hasn't caught the mouse. ☐
6 Kate is still in the gym. ☐
7 Steve hasn't painted the chair yet. ☐
8 My friends were chefs six years ago. ☐

3   Write three true sentences and one false sentence about yourself. Use *already, yet, just* or *for* and the ideas below or your own ideas.

2007 ....
six months ....
study English ....
live in this town ....
finish my homework ....

Unit 6

1 **Read, choose and complete.**

because   hadn't   ~~already~~   just   When   before   By   had   by

1 Ken had ...already... watched the film by the time his sister got home.
2 .... Jake got to the cafe the others had finished lunch.
3 Alan had .... crashed his car when the police arrived.
4 .... Wednesday James hadn't started his revision.
5 Barbara .... taken some great photos after the wedding.
6 Jodie hadn't eaten .... the party.
7 Elle was very angry .... Simon had broken her phone.
8 Ron was very tired because he .... slept.
9 The boys had planted a tree .... the time Sheila got home.

2 **Look at exercise 1 again. Write three questions. Ask your friend.**
1 *What had Jake's friends done?* ....
2 *What hadn't James done ?* ....
3 ....
4 ....
5 ....

3 **Choose and write the best ending for each sentence.**
1 Sarah went to her friend's house *after she had washed her hair* ....
2 Paul was in hospital ....
3 Gill had finished reading her book ....
4 The girls hadn't seen a tiger ....
5 I had left my bag at home ....
6 By the time the police arrived ....
7 Danny hadn't eaten lunch ....

a ...so he was very hungry.
b ...the burglar had run away.
c ...before they went to the zoo.
d ...so I didn't have any money.
e ...because he had broken his leg.
f ...after she had washed her hair.
g ...by dinner time.

Unit 7

1 **Write a sentence in each box. Use capital letters.**

After school	Next summer	When I'm 20
....	....	....

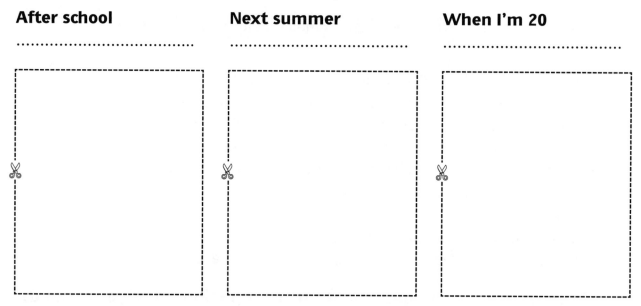

2 **Cut the sentences out. Play the guessing game in a group of four.**

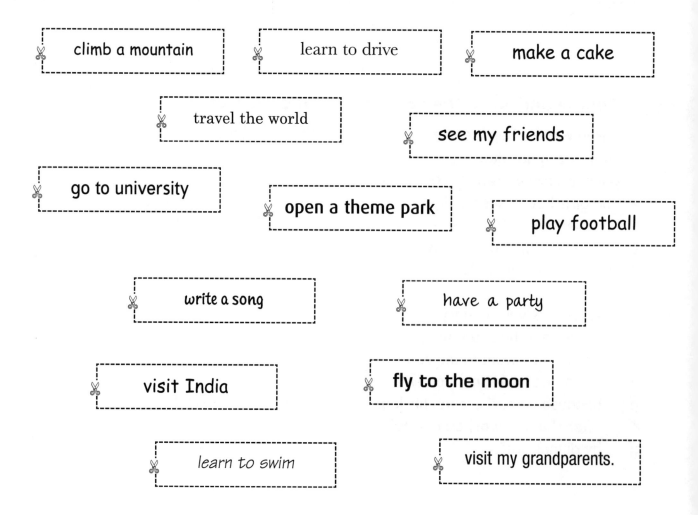

climb a mountain

learn to drive

make a cake

travel the world

see my friends

go to university

open a theme park

play football

write a song

have a party

visit India

fly to the moon

learn to swim

visit my grandparents.

Unit 8

1 Read and write.

You have just opened a fairground. Work with a partner and make eight rules for visitors. Use *can / can't, must / mustn't* and *have / don't have to*.

_____ *Fairground*

1 <u>You must wear a seatbelt on the rides.</u>

2 _____

3 _____

4 _____

5 _____

6 _____

7 _____

8 _____

2 Tell the class. Vote for the best rules.

Unit 9

1 Match.

1 You should

2 Take a drink because

3 You shouldn't run

4 We could go

5 It's raining so

6 You can't be

7 I may stay in bed

across the road.

I may not go to the park.

bring a camera.

cold because it's a hot day.

as I don't feel well.

you might get thirsty.

swimming after lunch.

2 Write the sentences out. Circle the modal verbs.

1 You *should* bring a camera ....

2 ....

3 ....

4 ....

5 ....

6 ....

7 ....

3 Work with a partner. Read and talk about what to do. Use the words in bold.

1 Your friend has a cold. Talk about what they **should/shouldn't** do.

2 Your parents aren't at home. Talk about where they **might** be.

3 It's Saturday tomorrow. Talk about what you **could** do.

4 Your friend has played football all morning. Talk about how he **must** feel.

Now write sentences.

1 You should drink hot water with lemon and honey ....

2 ....

3 ....

4 ....

Unit 10

1 **Write *offer* or *suggestion* after each sentence.**

1 Can I help you pack the clothes?   *offer* ....

2 Let's go to the mountains at the weekend.   ....

3 Shall we look at the map?   ....

4 Would you like an ice-cream?   ....

5 Why don't we go to Italy this year?   ....

6 I'll help you tidy the room.   ....

2 **Write.**

You are going to spend the weekend with your friend. Think about things you would like to do. Make suggestions and offers.

Let's... *go to the theatre.* ....

Why don't we... ....

Shall I... ....

What about... ....

Would you like... ....

We could... ....

How about... ....

3 **Talk to your friend. Use these phrases to help you answer.**

That's a good idea.

No, I don't like. ...

Yes, OK.

Oh, no. I hate. ...

Yes, please.

It's OK, I'll ...

4 **Agree to do three things. Tell the class.**

Unit 11

1 **Match and write sentences.**

If I eat cheese,	ask her to phone me.
He'll go to university	I am happy.
If I found £50,	if he passes his exams.
If you see Becky,	I feel sick.
I wouldn't eat so much	if we don't leave now.
We'll miss the show	if I were you.
When it's sunny,	I'd buy a new dress.

1 If I eat cheese, I feel... ....

2 ....

3 ....

4 ....

5 ....

6 ....

7 ....

2 **Write three wishes.**

1 I wish I were a pilot ....

2 ....

3 ....

4 ....

3 **Now write what you would do if your wishes came true.**

1 If I were a pilot, I would fly to China ....

2 ....

3 ....

4 ....

Unit 12

1 **Look and complete the sentences.**

1  There are three ..*pizzas*.... in the fridge.

2  The .... are falling off the trees now.

3 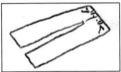 They have both got very short ....

4  Both these pairs of .... are great!

5  How many .... have we got?

6 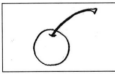 Look! There are lots of .... in the river.

7  We need to buy some more ....

8  I can see two .... taking the furniture to the van.

2 **Read and complete with *a / an* or *the*.**

David Black is [1] ..*an*....... English boy but he lives in [2] .... Italian town called Ferrara. His father is [3] .... doctor and his mother is [4] .... actress. They've got [5] .... beautiful flat in Venice.

They stay in [6] .... flat four times [7] .... year. Harry loves Venice but this year he is going to Egypt to see [8] .... pyramids.

Unit 13

A

1 **Read the instructions and complete the table for yourself.**

How much / many of these things do you have every day?

Put two ticks for *a lot.*
Put one tick for *not much / many.*
Put a cross for *not any.*

	Me	My partner
fruit		
glasses of water		
chocolate		
biscuits		
fish		
vegetables		

2 **Now ask your partner.**

3 **Write about your partner.**

.... eats a lot of .... but she doesn't eat much ....
....

✂ ··

B

1 **Read the instructions and complete the table for yourself.**

How much / many of these things do you have every day?

Put two ticks for *a lot.*
Put one tick for *not much / many.*
Put a cross for *not any.*

	Me	My partner
fruit		
glasses of water		
chocolate		
biscuits		
fish		
vegetables		

2 **Now ask your partner.**

3 **Write about your partner.**

.... eats a lot of .... but she doesn't eat much ....
....

52

Unit 14

ostrich penguin	Brad Pitt Harrison Ford	bike skateboard	golf tennis
April July September	elephant giraffe lion	Australia Egypt Canada	horse mouse dog
London Paris Amsterdam	lemonade cola orange juice	whale shark	Eiffel Tower Empire State Building

Unit 15

1 **Find and write the questions.**

| Did Gerry have guitar lessons? | Where are you going, Jack? |

| What are they doing? | ~~What happened?~~ | Can I help you? |

| Shall I turn the cooker off? | Did they have fun at the water park? |

1 _What happened?_

She went to the hospital by herself.
She went to the hospital by myself.

2 ....

They're testing ourselves.
They're testing each other.

3 ....

No, it's okay. We'll do it ourselves.
No, it's okay. We'll do it yourselves.

4 ....

I'm going for a walk by myself.
I'm going for a walk by himself.

5 ....

No, he taught himself.
No, he taught itself.

6 ....

Yes, they really enjoyed themselves.
Yes, they really enjoyed ourselves.

7 ....

It's okay, it will go off by yourself.
It's okay, it will go off by itself.

2 **Circle the correct answer.**

3 **Write three questions for your friend to answer.**

1 .... ?
2 .... ?
3 .... ?

Unit 16

1 **Read and complete.**

carefully   harder   fastest   better   older   easiest   good   worst   seriously

Dear Becky,

How are things? I'm studying for my exams and my brother is helping. I'm a year ¹ ...*older*... than Sam, but he's a lot ² .... at maths. It's my ³ .... subject! I will have to work much ⁴ .... next year.

I love English – it's my ⁵ .... subject but I take it very ⁶ .... I listen ⁷ .... in class and I always do my homework. My best friend at school is Angie. She's not as ⁸ .... as me so I help her after school.

Angie and Denise go to the school sports club and I want to join too. Denise is the ⁹ .... runner in my Year. I'm good but Denise always wins in school races!

Write soon with all your news.

Ella.

2 **Answer the questions.**

1 Who is younger than Ella?   *Sam* ....
2 What's Ella's worst subject?   ....
3 Which subject does she take very seriously?   ....
4 Who is Ella's best friend?   ....
5 Who is the fastest runner in Ella's year?   ....

3 **Write three questions for your friend to answer.**

1 .... ?
2 .... ?
3 .... ?

Unit 17

on	into
in front of	along
near	round
at	of

corner	maths
chair	vampires
police station	hospital
Wednesday	beach

behind	onto
next to	down
between	over
at	about

swimming	weekend
dog	supermarket
bridge	stairs
party	table

in	at
under	up
across	for
opposite	out of

bed	chemist
road	tree
chocolate	December
4 o'clock	window

Unit 18

1 **Write sentences.**

1 were laughing
the clown
at
they
.........They were laughing at the clown......... .

2 some bread
forgot
he
to get
....

3 to the concert
are going
after lunch
we
....

4 bought
Jack
she
some magazines
....

5 their
showed
me
new house
they
....

6 on holiday
I'm
next week
going
....

7 to
my best dress
Julie
I
lent
....

8 at 3 o'clock
we
basketball
are playing
....

2 **Take turns with your partner to make sentences.**

1 .....is playing.......... .....Lucy is playing tennis at 4 o'clock.................. .

2 meeting Lucy.......... ....

3 doesn't like.......... ....

4 went yesterday.......... ....

3 **Now write your own sentences.**

....
....
....

Unit 19

1 **Complete each question. Find and write the answer.**

1 Chloe: *Did* .... you have a great birthday?
  Beth: *Yes, I did* ....

2 Chloe: .... present did you like most?
  Beth: ....

3 Chloe: .... gave you the tickets?
  Beth: ....

4 Chloe: .... did you see at the concert?
  Beth: ....

5 Chloe: .... was the concert?
  Beth: ....

6 Chloe: .... did you get there?
  Beth: ....

7 Chloe: .... did you go with?
  Beth: ....

8 Chloe: .... it a good concert?
  Beth: ....

9 Chloe: .... people were there?
  Beth: ....

10 Chloe: .... your mum like Duffy?
  Beth: ....

In London.

Yes, it was brilliant!

I went with Mum and Hannah.

Yes, I did.

Over 20,000.

Tickets for a concert.

Duffy – she's a great singer!

Mum and Dad.

No, she didn't.

By train.

2 **Ask your partner questions about their birthday. Use the questions in exercise 1 to help you.**

.... ?
.... ?
.... ?
.... ?
.... ?
.... ?
.... ?
.... ?

Unit 20

1 Rewrite the sentences adding question tags.

1 You're from Italy.
You're from Italy, aren't you?

2 Sally can't drive.

....

3 They didn't go to the art class today.

....

4 Let's watch the game.

....

5 I'm good at making cakes.

....

6 He's got brown hair.

....

7 Stop playing that music.

....

8 Mum's going to buy a new TV.

....

9 Eating lots of fruit is good for you.

....

2 Work with a partner. Take turns to agree with the statements.

A: I don't like watching football.

B: Neither do I.

I'm going to learn to ski.

I've got a lot of CDs.

I didn't go shopping yesterday.

I went on holiday last summer.

I haven't finished my homework yet.

My dad doesn't play any instruments.

I want some chocolate.

Unit 21

1 Work with your friend. Match and complete the sentences.

The Eiffel Tower was (build)   about 2000 years ago.
Yoghurt is (make)   by Shakespeare.
Over 60 languages are (speak)   by farmers.
Paper was (invent)   from milk.
Sunflowers and *Starry Night* were (paint)   every minute.
One hundred iPods are (sell)   in 1889.
Macbeth was (write)   in Mexico.
Fruit and vegetables are (grow)   by Van Gogh.

2 Write the sentences in full.

1 *The Eiffel Tower was built in 1889* ....
2 ....
3 ....
4 ....
5 ....
6 ....
7 ....
8 ....

3 Write six more sentences using the prompts.

1 *The telephone* .... was invented by *Alexander Graham Bell* .

2 .... were sung by ....

3 .... is written by ....

4 .... are grown in ....

5 .... was painted by ....

6 .... are made in ....

Unit 22

1 **Work with a partner. Take turns to rewrite the sentences.**

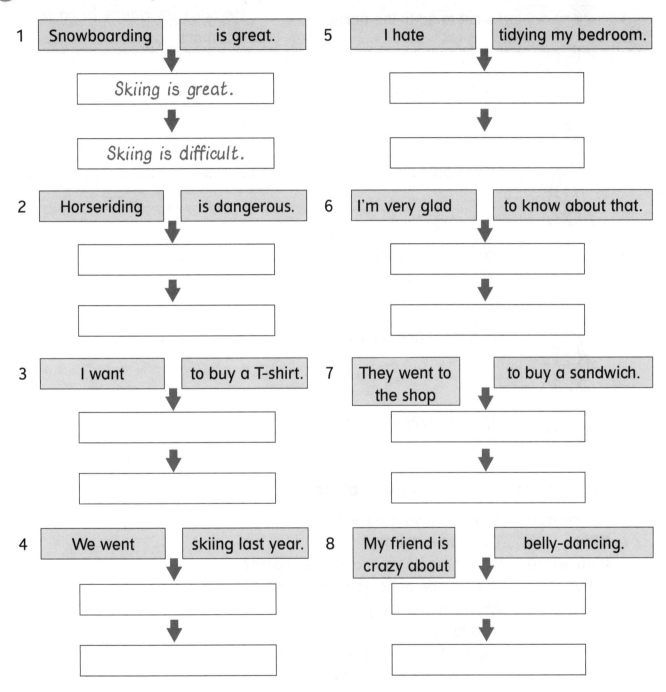

1 | Snowboarding | | is great. |

Skiing is great.

Skiing is difficult.

2 | Horseriding | | is dangerous. |

3 | I want | | to buy a T-shirt. |

4 | We went | | skiing last year. |

5 | I hate | | tidying my bedroom. |

6 | I'm very glad | | to know about that. |

7 | They went to the shop | | to buy a sandwich. |

8 | My friend is crazy about | | belly-dancing. |

2 **Rewrite this sentence as many times as you can.**

| I love |

| eating Italian food. |

Unit 23

1 **Report what the speakers say.**

1   I want to go to the party.   *He says he wants to go to the party* .

2   I've got to do lots of homework.   ....

                             ....

3   I love apple pie.   ....

                             ....

4   I can't run very fast.   ....

                             ....

5   I'm hungry and thirsty.   ....

                             ....

6   My sister lives in Spain.   ....

                             ....

2 **Write a report of the conversation.**

Policeman:	Where are your parents?
Billy:	They are at home.
Policeman:	What time do you have to go home?
Billy:	I have to be at home by 9'oclock.
Policeman:	What's in your bag?
Billy:	It's a duck.
Policeman:	You can't carry a duck in a bag.
Billy:	It's okay – it's a toy duck.

Yesterday a policeman stopped Billy in the street.

The policeman asked ... *where Billy's parents were* ....

Billy said ....

The policeman wanted to know ....

Billy said ....

....

....

....

Unit 24

1 **Complete the puzzles. Write the missing name and *who, which, that* or *whose*.**

1 An ..*umbrella*.......... is something ..*which / that*... we can use in the rain.

2 A .... is a person .... works in a bakery.

3 A .... is an animal .... neck is very long.

4 A .... is a person .... looks after sick animals.

5 A .... is a shop .... sells meat.

6 A .... is an insect .... wings have bright colours.

2 **Finish the sentences.**

1 A cat is ..*a small animal that likes to chase mice*... .

2 A glass is ....

3 A nurse is ....

4 A ball is ....

5 An Italian is ....

6 A lion is ....

3 **Write four more sentence openers.**

1 ....

2 ....

3 ....

4 ....

4 **Ask your partner to complete the sentences.**

Unit 25

1 **Choose subjects from Box A and write sentences using linking words from Box B.**

A	
sport	animals
school	languages
food	family
film	music
weather	friends

B	
but	because
and	although
so	

1 *She isn't in the school team although she's really good at tennis* .
2 ....
3 ....
4 ....
5 ....

2 **Write your own story. Use all the linking words from Box B in exercise 1.**

Photocopiable © Pearson Education Limited 2008